Why We Give

Why We Give

Tim Milner

Published in San Francisco, CA

San Francisco, CA

Abbreviated version originally published in 2012. Expanded and republished in 2014.

Printed in the USA

ISBN 9781503246768

Unless otherwise indicated, Scripture is quoted from the English Standard Version of the Bible.

Contents

To my Dad, Tom Milner, for showing me how to trust God not only with my soul, but also with my money.

Intro: **Why**

*For it will be like a man going on a journey, who
called his servants and entrusted to them his
property.*

-Matthew 25:14

Jesus spoke more about money, than any other
topic except the Kingdom of Heaven. Let that
sink in. Jesus knows money is important. But, it
may not be important for the reasons you think
it's important. Money is important because what
you do with your money is simply an overflow of
what you believe about God.

Not only did Jesus talk plainly about money,
but He also told stories about money. Jesus was
the ultimate storyteller. He could illustrate deep
and important truths simply, through stories
known as parables. At one point, Jesus tells a
parable of a Master, who represents God. In this
particular parable, there are also three servants.
Near the end of the parable the Master says to
two of the servants, *Well done, good and faithful
servant!* To the third, however, he says, *You
wicked and slothful servant.* What was the

difference between those who the Master praised, and the one who he condemned? The difference was in how they used what they were given.

Most of us have been given much. It's our responsibility to learn what we are to do with it. If we don't, we risk not living the life God intended for us.

One of the things we have been entrusted with is financial resources. God intended that we be generous with the resources He has given us. And yet, many of us aren't being generous with our resources in the way that we could be. Sometimes it's because we don't know or understand what's asked of us. Sometimes we know, but think the rules are antiquated or outdated. And sometimes we just think we know better.

But as we begin to explore why we give, we quickly learn that there are many reasons to give. One of the beautiful things about Jesus' teaching is how deep and rich it is.

The two servants in the parable who were praised knew exactly what to do. They knew their Master expected them to get a good return on the resources that He entrusted to them. Likewise, it's conceivable that the misbehaving servant did not know why the Master had entrusted him with resources in the first place.

In this book we'll learn why we should wisely use the money God has put us in charge of, and don't worry – we'll also talk about how.

Money is a huge part of a Christian's life. However, when it comes to money, many people still act frighteningly similar to the way they lived before following Jesus. It shouldn't be this way.

What if you could take several hours this week to finally learn what God intended for you and your money? What if you could make an investment of only a few hours by reading through the reasons why we should give?

At the *very* least, you would then know what you are saying no to – if you disagree. However, on the other hand, a small investment of time reading through this book will pay huge dividends as you learn why we give. It'll change your life, and the life of others in this lifetime, and for all eternity. Sounds like a big promise? These are the types of claims that Jesus makes about giving. One of my favorite passages on giving is found in Luke 16:1-13. In the first half of the chapter, we see that Jesus is challenging us to use our resources strategically on things that will change other people's eternity.

Jesus makes the point that people act strategically all the time for things that ultimately don't really matter. What if we could give the same amount of attention, focus, and strategic thought to things that will impact eternity? What if you spent some time thinking through how you can use your resources to promote Jesus? Think of the difference it could make.

A sobering truth is that most of us are genuinely confused about what Jesus and the Biblical authors wrote on giving. That's unfortunate, because there is a lot at stake.

I'd ask that you read this book with an expectation that you will be making an investment in something that will change the course of your life. Making this investment will most likely change the lives of people around you as well. Through the course of this book, we'll learn a number of different principles that we can apply to the ways that we handle our money. We'll learn why, how, when and where we should be generous. But most importantly, we'll see what God says about money in the Bible, and how learning why we give is an invitation to a closer relationship with God, and a more joyful, fulfilled life.

1. **Submission**

The reason why many are still troubled, still seeking, still making little forward progress is because they haven't yet come to the end of themselves. We're still trying to give orders, and interfering with God's work within us.

-A.W. Tozer

It was a Sunday evening in 2012 and Ben Pilgreen and I were taking a red-eye to Atlanta. We were attending a conference and it began the next morning. Not wanting to miss our Sunday night service at Epic, we caught the midnight plane. The plan was that we would sleep on the plane and wake up refreshed ready to attend three exciting days of conferences.

That was the plan.

About forty-five minutes into the flight, I awoke to the overwhelming feeling of sickness. You know, *that* feeling. Nausea overtook me in waves. I was about to lose it. I didn't know *exactly how* it was going to come out, but it was about to come out. I elbowed Ben, who was already sleeping like a baby. (I don't get how people can sleep on planes.) Earlier in the week my wife Kristin had been sick with a stomach bug. So being the hypochondriac that I am, I had packed Pepto Bismol - just in case. I shouted to Ben, "Get me my Pepto. It's in my bag." He says, "Okay." But unfortunately, he falls back to sleep immediately. Plan A failed.

Time to go to plan B. I was sitting in the middle seat. When Ben and I fly, he always makes me take the middle. (One day I'll write a book on submission, and I will bring this back up.) So, I climbed over him and started running to the lavatory, as they are always called on planes. Now at this point I don't want to come off as crude or gross, but I need you to re-live this with me. As I approached the lavatory, I fell to my knees. I'm still not really sure how what is in my stomach is going to come out, but now I'm thinking it's coming up through the mouth.

On my knees I push in the doors to the lavatory with one hand - because all lavatory doors on planes have to be pushed in the center to open. While pushing the door open with one hand, I notice the flight attendant out of the corner of my eye. She is in her jump seat. She is asleep. At this point, I'm leaning over and with my free arm I hit her on the shoulder. In a state of panic about to throw up at 30,000 feet, I did what anyone in my situation would do. I ordered a Coke.

I thought it would help. I think it did help.

So I sat there on the floor of the lavatory going 550 miles per hour towards Atlanta at 30,000 feet. I'm so thankful I was one of the first people to use the lavatory on this trip. The floor was still kind of clean.

That's when I officially met her. She came in like a lady-knight riding a white horse - carrying my Coke. She was the friendliest grandmother type of person you could ever imagine. She asked me what was wrong.

And I made what would go down as one of the greater aviation mistakes of 2012. I told her I was wheezy. Now, if you've spent much time with me, you know I occasionally get in a hurry and spout off a word that, though similar, is not the word I meant. Sometimes I catch it, and sometimes I'm actually confused about the meaning. In this situation, I was genuinely confused about the meaning of the word wheezy.

She said, "You're wheezy?!" (notice the exclaiming voice that I just wrote with). I said, "Yes but I think I'll be fine." She told me to lay down flat, and asked if I was having a hard time breathing. I said, "No, I'm just wheezy." She responded, "You can't breathe?!" I said, "NO! I'm *just* wheezy!" At this point *all* the flight attendants are circling around me. Each asking varying questions, but almost all the questions centering on me not breathing. At one point, my original grandmother-knight-in-armor flight attendant had a phone in her hand, leans over me, looks me in the eye, and says, "I've got the captain on the phone. Do we need to land this plane?"

Queasy. Not wheezy. They sound very similar, but they are very different.

After a while I was finally able to calm everyone down, and by avoiding the word wheezy I was able to convince everyone that I had a stomach problem, not a breathing problem. For the remainder of that flight the grandmother-like hero woman took good care of me. Ends up she had worked many years as a nurse and knew just what to do in these situations. She would tell me to stop drinking Coke. Start drinking ginger ale. Do this, don't do that. The rest of the plane was still in normal mode. (There's actually another story in here, but for sake of time, I have to skip it.) She had to take care of them with refreshments, but I was her special patient for the rest of the flight. She took care of me, and I trusted her.

Looking back, I can laugh at it now. Sorry if it grossed you out. I just needed you to understand the situation. I was in humble circumstances and looking for someone to lead me. She answered the call for help and I was grateful. Anything she told me to do, I did. Somehow, almost immediately after our first meeting, I submitted to her leading. Anything she said, I did. Submitting is obeying. And I obeyed her every command quite willingly, because I needed help and she seemed to know exactly what to do.

Do you see where I'm about to go with this?

Before we go any further, I need to ask are you willing to do whatever God asks of you? When we hear of submission today it usually has negative connotations. Our minds often begin thinking about having to obey someone else's rules, or having to do things we *really* don't want to do because we are forced to. But can submission be a good thing? I sure hope so! It helped me survive that plane ride.

But on a more serious note, Paul would frequently use words to describe his submission to Christ. Paul was willing to do whatever God asked him to do. In fact, Paul opens up his letter, *Romans*, as *Paul, a servant of Christ...* When looking at that same phrase in the original Greek, other translations of the Bible would say that the word *servant* may be better translated *slave*.

Romans 12:2 states, *And do not be conformed to this world, but be transformed by the renewing of your mind, so that you may prove what the will of God is, that which is good and acceptable and perfect.* As we submit to Christ and His will, over time we will become more like Him. As we become more like Him, we will increasingly learn that His ways are good, acceptable and perfect. We learn that the more we submit to His ways, the better our lives become.

In the Bible we also see others talk about submitting to Christ. Peter, one of Jesus' disciples, says, *Humble yourselves, therefore, under the mighty hand of God so that at the proper time he may exalt you...* (1 Peter 5:6).

Furthermore, James 4:7, says, *Submit yourselves therefore to God.* Some of my personal favorite verses about submitting to God come from the Psalms. Psalm 40:8 says, *I delight to do Your will, O my God; Your Law is within my heart.* Psalms 143:10 reads, *Teach me to do Your will, For You are my God; Let Your good Spirit lead me on level ground.*

Psalms also offers a warning to those who do not submit to God's will. *But my people did not listen to my voice; Israel would not submit to me. So I gave them over to their stubborn hearts, to follow their own counsels. Oh, that my people would listen to me, that Israel would walk in my ways!* (Psalm 81:11-13).

Finally, Jesus had a lot to say about submitting to the Father's will as well.   In Matthew 6:10, He teaches us to pray, *Your kingdom come. Your will be done, on earth as it is in heaven.*

What does it mean *Your will be done?* It means that Christ was teaching us to seek God's will for all areas of our life - including His will for how we are to use our money.

The moment we place our faith in Christ, it is our business to begin submitting to God and His ways. I love Epic Church's vision statement, *To see an increasing number of people in San Francisco orienting their entire lives around Jesus.* This vision statement really gets to the heart of what it looks like to submit to God - orienting our *entire* lives around His will.

In the rest of this book we will explore why we give and why it's important for all who follow Christ. But before we continue, can you agree that once you know God's will that you will submit to it? *I can tell you personally that I have never submitted to God's will and then regretted it.* Anytime I have decided to do it God's way, I've always been more than satisfied with the outcome. I'm not saying it's always been easy, but I am saying it has always been best.

Submission Recap

❖ The Apostle Paul considered himself a slave to Christ (in a good way).

❖ God's will is good, acceptable and perfect - Romans 12:2.

❖ Psalms 40:8 says, *I delight to do Your will, O my God...*

❖ There are negative consequences when we resist God's will – Psalms 81:11-13.

❖ Christians need to seek God's will in all areas of their life.

❖ I've personally never regretted doing it God's way.

Submission Discussion Questions

❖ In this chapter what was the most helpful for you?

❖ What does submission mean to you?

❖ Are you willing to submit to God's will? If so, why? Or, why not?

❖ How can you discover God's will?

❖ Has there ever been a time when you've done something God's way but regretted it?

❖ Describe a time when you did something God's way and you didn't regret it?

❖ What other references in the Bible do you know of that talk about submitting to God?

❖ Which Bible verse about submitting to God did you find most helpful or interesting? Why?

❖ What area(s) of your life do you need to orient around Christ?

❖ Describe specifically how submitting to God relates to giving.

2. **Steward**

Well done, good and faithful servant. You have been faithful over a little; I will set you over much.

-Matthew 25:21

It was 2009, and I was a junior in college. Like most juniors in college I was not particularly great at listening. I was especially bad at keeping up with the family updates that my mom told me over the phone. To say I wasn't great at it is an understatement. It would have been one thing if I zoned out of one conversation here or there, but sometimes I would go months without really comprehending a single word that I heard. Am I exaggerating? Keep reading.

Now before I go any further, I need mom to look at this footnote[1]. Everyone else keep your eyes up here. You looked, didn't you? It's okay. Back to the story. So, one particular Friday night I made my quarterly trip home from college. I arrived at my mom's house just a little after dinner. It was beginning to get dark. I drove up

---

[1] Mom, I'm much better at listening now, I promise!

and parked my car in my usual parking spot near the carport. I went to the backdoor, unlocked it with my key, went to the fridge and grabbed a Coke. No one else was home, or at least mom's car wasn't here. But, I'm a man who pays attention to details. So, after years of picking up on their social patterns, I know they will be home soon because they are rarely away from home past dark. I take my can of soda and head to the living room to watch TV until they arrive. Then we could start the customary catch up of the last three months that usually involved a lot of laughing. And I mean a lot of laughing. But there would be no laughing at this catch up. Well, maybe there would be, but the loosely planned catch up time with mom wasn't about to happen in this living room, or this house, or even this neighborhood.

As I stood in the living room about to begin my search for the remote control, I noticed something. This is not mom's furniture. Mom doesn't have this kind of TV. Wait, these aren't pictures of me on the wall. These are some other kids I don't even know.

Panic.

I sat that soda down on some stranger's dinner table and ran out of there, called my mom, and asked where she was and what happened to her house.

27

She had moved. And she had been telling me about it for months. I am now a better listener.

That is embarrassing, and that really happened. But this story to some degree illustrates another alarming discovery I would make several years later. I thought that house was mine (at least in the sense that it was my mom's) and I thought that was my Coke and that I was free to use it however I liked. I thought all of my mom's house was at my disposal. But wow, did I get that one wrong. And just like that embarrassing night, I discovered that all the things that I thought were mine were actually someone else's as well.

Everything I own is actually God's.

Does God allow me to use the things He has given me? Yes. But, I realized that "my" things were on loan.

When I discovered this, I didn't panic but I did begin to take steps in making sure that I was using the things I had been loaned in a way that would please the God who truly owned them. It's changed my life in incredible ways. So much so, I can't stop talking about and encouraging others to begin to honor God with His things that He is letting us use.

Therefore, take this subject seriously. Perhaps for the first time you can begin using what you've been given in a way that is in line with God's plan for you and your money. You can't use your money the way it is fully intended to be used unless you first understand that you are a steward. You are not the king or queen of your domain. God is. And the sooner we recognize that and reposition our life and our possessions accordingly, the better.

Have you ever asked yourself, "Why?" In a moment of skepticism or honest curiosity, have you ever wondered why you do the things you do? I have. And I still do daily. It can be a blessing and a curse. The Psalm *should* say, "There is no rest for the *curious*." At times I - and probably all of us - can resonate with this when we just have to know, why do we do this certain thing in a certain way.

An honest dose of skepticism and curiosity can also be a blessing. It often causes us to lead with conviction. When I know not only the *what*, the *how*, the *when*, and *where*, but when I also know the *why*, then I truly begin to understand it. It's when I know and understand the why that - if I find it agreeable - I can truly accept the thought, the idea, and the value, as my own.

Then I can own it. Then I can take it and run with it. Then I can be passionate about it. Then I can advocate for it. Then I can do my best to embody it.

That's what happened when I discovered why we give.

So what is the big idea behind giving? If you want to understand why giving is important, you must understand one word. Stewardship. Or managing. Or overseeing. Or custodian. Or caretaker. Or agent. Whichever word you want to use. And they all describe our relationship with our *stuff* perfectly.

When my daughter was two she thought everything in our house was hers. Well, there is a tad of truth in there somewhere. But it's not the whole story. Not even close. Sophia has permission to use almost anything she sees - except for that which would be dangerous or counterproductive to her development. But she doesn't own any of it. Her mother and I do. For most of it I could actually find the receipts.

And to take this example one step further, I don't own all the things Sophia sees. I steward it. Our house, all those items I can show you receipts for, our retirement account, our savings account, our vehicle, everything I have I'm stewarding. It's God's. Everything. There is nothing that I can point to and say with certainty that that is mine. Everything I have is on loan from God. One of my roles here on earth is to steward what God has blessed me with in such a way that it pleases God. But if you do not understand that everything you have is on borrow from God then the rest of this book will sound, well, to be honest, *optional*.

Do you believe me that we are all stewards, not truly owners? Let's take a look at several passages from the Bible.

My favorite passage on stewardship is Matthew 25:14-30. It's a long passage, but it's my favorite for a reason. Read it with me.

For it will be like a man going on a journey, who called his servants and entrusted to them his property. To one he gave five talents, to another two, to another one, to each according to his ability. Then he went away. He who had received the five talents went at once and traded with them, and he made five talents more. So also he who had the two talents made two talents more. But he who had received the one talent went and dug in the ground and hid his master's money. Now after a long time the master of those servants came and settled accounts with them. And he who had received the five talents came forward, bringing five talents more, saying, "Master, you delivered to me five talents; here I have made five talents more." His master said to him, "Well done, good and faithful servant. You have been faithful over a little; I will set you over much. Enter into the joy of your master." And he also who had the two talents came forward, saying, "Master, you delivered to me two talents; here I have made two talents more." His master said to him, "Well done, good and faithful servant. You have been faithful over a little; I will set you over much. Enter into the joy of your master." He also who had received the one talent came forward, saying, "Master, I knew you to be a hard man, reaping where you did not sow, and gathering where you scattered no seed, so I was afraid, and I went and hid your talent in the ground. Here you have what is yours." But his master answered him, "You wicked and slothful servant! You knew that I reap where I have not sown and gather where I scattered no seed? Then you ought to have invested my money with the bankers, and at my coming I should have received what was my own with interest. So take the talent from him and give it to him who has the ten talents. For to everyone who has will more be given, and he will have an abundance. But from the one who has not, even what he has will be taken away. And cast the worthless servant into the outer darkness. In that place there will be weeping and gnashing of teeth."

Now to be fair, this parable is not exclusively talking about stewarding our bank account. In context, Jesus was warning His hearers to be prepared for when they would meet God face to face. Though the parable uses talents, which is money, as the example, the main point is that we must be faithful with *everything* that God has given us. This includes money, but it also includes the more important things, such as the truth and knowledge of God.

This passage teaches us some very important lessons about stewarding:

➢ God has given us so much! Keep in mind here that a *talent* is about fifty years wages for a laborer.

➢ God has given us each different amounts. This could be based upon how we stewarded in the past, or we could look at it that God will not give us more than we can properly steward.

➢ Everything we steward comes from the Master.

➢ We are given a great deal of freedom to steward how we see fit.

➢ God will one day have us give an account to how we steward what He gave us.

➢ There will be blessings for those who steward well.

➢ There will be punishment for those who do not steward well.

From this passage are we given any clues as to what good stewardship looks like? Yes! We are told that those who did a good job were faithful with what they were given. We are told that they also multiplied what they were given. So, how can we be faithful, multiply and provide a good return on what our Master has given us? We will explore that in the rest of this book as well. But I can go ahead and give you a preview. *We are faithful; we multiply, and provide a good return on investment when we invest what God has given us into things that point people to Jesus.* Again, we'll go into greater detail in the chapters to follow, but let that marinate in your mind as we continue.

Before we leave this passage and move on, can we tell anything about what bad stewardship looks like? Again, the answer is yes. The bad steward didn't do anything (except hide) with what the master gave him. Perhaps the greater problem was that the servant didn't really know what the master expected. Of course, if someone gives you fifty year's wages and asks you to steward it, don't you think you should make sure you are absolutely clear on what is expected of you? Yes, you should.

In the same way today, we've been given so much by our Master, and we've also been asked to steward it. So shouldn't we make sure we are absolutely clear on what God expects us to do with what He has given us to steward? Yes. I would go as far as to say that God has made it very clear what He expects from us as stewards. The Bible is full of examples. At this point, it's on you as a steward to seek understanding of what God expects from you. So, let's continue with a few more passages helping us to see the Biblical idea of stewardship.

The earth is the Lord's and the fullness thereof, the world and those who dwell therein... (Psalm 24:1). We can see in this passage that the world and everything in it belongs to God.

The Israelites in the Old Testament were not supposed to be allowed to sell land (at least not the way we understand it today). When someone "bought" land, they were simply buying the right to use the land. The only true landowner is God. *The land shall not be sold in perpetuity, for the land is mine. For you are strangers and sojourners with me* (Leviticus 25:23).

Well at least I own *me*? Not so fast. *Or do you not know that your body is a temple of the Holy Spirit within you, whom you have from God? You are not your own, for you were bought with a price. So glorify God in your body* (1 Corinthians 6:19-20).

All things are Christ's. He made them, He sustains them, and all things belong to Christ. We simply steward them. *For from him and through him and to him are all things. To him be glory forever. Amen* (Romans 11:36).

It's easy to make the argument that what we own is ours, because we were the ones who put in the hard work. We were the ones who wisely made this decision or that. We were the ones who interviewed well for the job. We were the ones who climbed the corporate ladder. We were the ones who saw an opportunity to sell a product.

Again, have you considered where those ideas, ambitions, opportunities, and even the thoughts and ideas that lead to your successes come from? *You shall remember the Lord your God, for it is he who gives you power to get wealth, that he may confirm his covenant that he swore to your fathers, as it is this day* (Deuteronomy 8:18).

You are managing what God has blessed you with. But most of us act like it's our stuff and we do exactly what we want with it - not knowing that we are missing out on a huge blessing. Not only are we missing out on a blessing, but we may be dangerously close to the example of the steward who *hid* what his Master gave him.

Every single day most of us make financial decisions. Did you know that financial decisions are often spiritual decisions? Does the way you use your money reflect that you are stewarding someone else's resources? Or does it reflect the façade that it's all yours and you can use it however you want without consequence?

Before ending this chapter, we must first ask ourselves, do we trust God, the rightful owner of our things? Our answer will determine how good of a steward we can ultimately become.

Lee Iaccoa said that *decisiveness is the one word that makes a good manager.* Once we decide we can trust God with the resources He has given us to manage, then we must act *decisively* by stewarding well.

Steward Recap

❖ We are not owners. We are stewards.

❖ We have been given a great deal of freedom in how we steward.

❖ The Bible teaches us how God wants us to steward our resources.

❖ There are great rewards for stewarding well.

❖ If you are not wisely stewarding the resources God has blessed you with, you are missing out on huge blessings in both this life and in eternity.

❖ It's on you to learn how God intends for you to steward the resources He has given you.

Steward Discussion Questions

❖ In this chapter what was the most helpful for you?

❖ What is a steward?

❖ What evidence do we have that we are stewards and not owners of all that we have?

❖ Which Bible passage resonated with you the most about stewardship? Why?

❖ What will we do differently if we begin to see things as a steward instead of an owner?

❖ Has there ever been a time in your life when you discovered that what you thought you had control over, ended up being untrue?

❖ What advantages are there that what we thought we owned, is actually owned by God?

❖ What's one thing you could do today, to become a better steward?

3. **Imitator**

Be imitators of God as dear children.

-Apostle Paul, *Ephesians* 5:3

I really wanted the title of this book to be *The Giver*. Unfortunately, that name was already taken. Thanks a lot Lois Lowry. (Had I got to the title first, I probably could have sold 10 million copies too.) That title would have been perfect for this book. And quite frankly, Lowry should have titled her book *The Receiver*, but I digress. Come to think of it, maybe I should have named this book, *The Receiver*. That would have been perfect. I could have talked about how much we've received and in return we should then be givers.

Shoot.

Oh well, it's too late. *Why We Give* it is. On a more serious note, why would *The Giver* be a good title for this book? Because God is a giver and we are called to imitate Him.

The Bible is a book of giving. In the broadest terms, the Bible is a beautiful story of God's plan for mankind. It starts with God creating everything perfectly, and then *giving* it to man to use. Then we see that man sinned against God. Because man sinned against God, we deserved to die as punishment. But what did God do? He paid the price for us by *giving* His son Jesus to die in our place. The Bible teaches that if we follow Jesus, He will *give* us new life and we will do away with the old life that left us empty and at odds with God. Finally, the Bible teaches that there will come a day when God will wipe away every problem. He will make all things right, the way they were intended to be before man sinned. Then, God and man will dwell together in eternity.

The entire Bible is a grand narrative where God gave man one thing after another, and man never deserved any of it. It's God's grace, and we see example after example, not only in the Scriptures, but also in our own lives. We have a generous God.

By reading through the Bible we can see that giving is at the heart of God. It's in His character. Once we see the heart of God, we can begin to model all areas of our life after our perfect and very generous God.

If we are going to follow God's example by becoming like Him in generosity, let's see what God teaches about giving. Interestingly enough, we don't have to look far for the first example of giving to God. We only have to look as far as the first book of the Bible, *Genesis*. We are told how Abraham pursues an army that seized his brother-in-law and his relatives. Abraham overtakes the captors and frees his family. Afterwards, Abraham gives ten percent of the spoils of war to Melchizedek, who was acting as the High Priest (Genesis 14:20). By giving to the High Priest, he in effect gave directly to God.

You're probably saying in your mind right now, "Tim, next time I overtake an army, I'll gladly give God ten percent of the spoils of war. But what does this have to do with me today?" Abraham knew that God had blessed him. He recognized that the riches and wealth he gained were a direct result of God's blessing. This is the first instance where we will see a theme of giving ten percent (also known as a tithe) to God. In the same way today, everything we receive comes from God. Out of gratitude and indebtedness, Abraham gave God ten percent.

Moses' Law

In the Old Testament, God gives Moses various laws to give to the Israelites. Here we see the tithe appear again and given with very clear instructions. *Every tithe of the land, whether of the seed of the land or of the fruit of the trees, is the Lord's; it is holy to the Lord* (Leviticus 27:3). In the Old Testament times, coined and paper money were not as widely used as they are today. Most people's wealth would have been in livestock, food, and land. Therefore, throughout the Old Testament when you see people giving a tithe, it is usually in the form of livestock or food.

In order for the Israelites to remember that *everything* they had came from God, God told them that one tenth of all things shall be dedicated to God, and declared holy.

There were two other tithes as well (Deuteronomy 14:22-29). These tithes were given for the purpose of worshipping, helping those in need, and taking care of the Levites (similar to the clergy today). Out of these additional two tithes, one was to be collected for two years in a row, and one was to be collected every third year. The Old Testament times were very different than times today, but for perspective, keep in mind that the Israelites were required to bring two tithes each year.

Through these required tithes, we see God's generous attributes. God sets up a system by which those who are serving Him vocationally (the Levities – or clergy today) are taken care of, and the needy (the traveler, the widow and the fatherless) in each town are well provided for. Furthermore, the second tithe referenced above was in many ways a vacation where the family would travel to a destination and worship. How would someone pay for this travel, especially in the times when Moses originally wrote this? God told them to save up ten percent of their income to cover the costs. Seriously, read Deuteronomy 14:22-26. It was a purposeful vacation in which the family would get away and spend time worshipping God; a welcomed relief for those who spent the rest of the year farming and raising livestock. Yes, God is very generous, and He takes care of those who trust Him.

The point is that the Israelites were told that everything they had was from God and that a portion of it was to be made holy and given back to God. When we do this, it reminds us that all we have comes from God.

Can a person rob God?

The book of Malachi, the last book of the Old Testament, is a book written for the Israelites, but is still very applicable for us to understand today. Essentially, the Israelites were cheating on their obligations towards God. They were not giving their best. They had become selfish towards each other and to God. They were not being faithful to each other, which God wanted, and they were not being faithful to God (and yes, God wanted this as well!). In Malachi 3, we learn that when they did bring God an offering, such as a lamb, they would, unfortunately, bring God the worst lamb in their flock.

God had asked for their best lamb.

Imagine you lived thousands of years ago and it was time to bring an offering to God. So you went to your flock to bring a lamb. You know that you are expected to bring your best lamb, but you see a sick lamb lying down, barely alive. You reason to yourself that the lamb is about to die soon anyways. Let's just bring the sick lamb to give to God. And that is exactly what the Israelites are accused of doing in the book of Malachi - bringing God their worst, not their best.

There was no faith or reverence in their offering. God tells them in Malachi 3 to bring their best to Him. It was clear what was expected of them, but they decided to bring their worst. In Malachi 3:8-12, God tells the Israelites:

> Can a person rob God? You indeed are robbing me, but you say, "How are we robbing you?" In tithes and contributions! You are bound for judgment because you are robbing me – this whole nation is guilty. "Bring the entire tithe into the storehouse so that there may be food in my temple. Test me in this matter," says the Lord who rules over all, "to see if I will not open for you the windows of heaven and pour out for you a blessing until there is no room for it all. Then I will stop the plague from ruining your crops, and the vine will not lose its fruit before harvest," says the Lord who rules over all. "All nations will call you happy, for you indeed will live in a delightful land," says the Lord who rules over all.

This is the only time throughout the Bible that God says in a positive way *test me.* He is saying bring your full tithe and *test me to see if I will not open for you the windows of heaven and pour out for you a blessing until there is no room for it all* (Malachi 3:10). God goes on to say that the plague that was ruining the crop and the vine losing its fruit will end. Few of us today have weak vines or plagued crops. In today's terms it wouldn't be vines or crops, but perhaps financial investments, real estate, and automobiles. This verse is not saying that if you give ten percent to God you will never have to repair your car again. But God's promise is clear that those who bring the full tithe will be taken care of. In the context of this passage, the blessing is not just internal and intangible, such as the peace of knowing you did what God has asked you to do. Here God is saying He will give you more to oversee if you will first trust Him enough to return the full ten percent back to Him.

How can I best steward God's additional blessing?

Throughout this book, whenever we come across a passage that promises great rewards, I want you to pause for just a moment. There are so many reasons why we are supposed to give back to God. However, if we only focus on giving so that we can receive a return, we are missing out on everything. And quite frankly, we may be disqualifying ourselves from the reward. It is undeniable that there are a vast number of verses in the Bible, both Old Testament and New Testament, that speak of the rewards for those who give. Rewards are part of giving. Sometimes the rewards we receive are non-financial. If they are financial (which is not uncommon) the purpose is not typically so that you can live in increasing comfort and luxury.

In the times when we are blessed financially, perhaps God blessed you because you were faithful with a little and now He wants to give you more resources so that you can continue to be faithful. Said differently, if God blesses you for giving, don't presume that the blessing was suppose to be a Christmas bonus, so to speak, that you can use on yourself however you want. Take the blessing and reinvest it back into God's Kingdom by giving generously. I'm not saying that if you get a raise you shouldn't consider using the added resources for a well needed vacation, a bigger home, or a car. What I am saying is that when you're blessed, take a moment to *selah* - which means to pause and reflect. As you think about the blessing you've received, ask yourself, "What is the best way I can steward this money?" We will talk a lot more about God's blessing and what we should do when He blesses us in chapter 7, *Blessed*.

Is money the only blessing?

As alluded to above, financial resources are *not* the only way God will bless you. Your faith will be blessed. Maybe your relationships will be blessed. There are a lot of ways God can bless you. In 2 Kings 4:8-37; 8:1-6, there is a great story where a woman gave to God. In this account, we see that God did not bless this already wealthy woman with more money; at least not yet. Instead, God blessed this woman and her husband with a child. They had wanted a child but the woman was barren. The woman's faith in giving towards the prophet of God resulted in her being blessed with the child she always wanted. Read the passage, it's in there.

Later in the book of 2 Kings, we see that the same woman was warned to flee the country because a very bad famine was about to hit. In that culture if she left her country, she would forfeit all the land she abandoned. But when the woman came back to her homeland, the king at that time gave her back all of her property without any trouble.

We see in this passage that the king's favor towards the woman came from God. In the end, God blessed this woman not only with the son she always wanted, protection from a great famine that could have killed her and her family, but also financially by giving her favor with the king. Are you being faithful in what you have? The woman in this story was furthering God's Kingdom and God blessed her for it.

What causes the blessing?

I believe this would be a good time to add that

the woman had God's favor, but not because she gave. The woman had God's favor because she loved and sought after God. Because the woman loved God, of course she gave generously. She understood that out of all the things she should have given her money to, she wanted to first give back to God. Jesus said where our treasure is, there our heart will be also (Matthew 6:21). She gave because she loved God. We would be missing the point if we believed that she was given a child, saved from the famine, and blessed financially only because she gave. She received all of those things because of God's favor. From what we see in the passage, I'm willing to bet that even if she was not given a child, even if she was directly affected by the drought, even if she lost everything financially, she would still love God. She would still continue to give generously towards the God she loved so much.

I'm not sure why you picked up this book, but I want to be sure you are clear. The Bible is full of God's blessings for those who trust Him. I do not believe the blessings are there as a way for us to gain more toys. I believe the promises are there so that we would learn to trust God. If you trust God in some areas of your life, but not all areas – like your money – you don't fully trust Him.

It's like a doctor telling you to lose twenty pounds.

What does that doctor have to gain by you losing weight? Nothing. He would actually probably make a lot more money if you stayed unhealthy. But the doctor tells you all the benefits of losing twenty pounds – you'll feel good, you'll look good, you'll live longer, etc. – to encourage you to just do it. The doctor knows it's in your best interest, and he wants to push you to do it. In the same way all the benefits of giving we find in the Bible are to encourage you to give generously, and maybe for the first time, trust God in all areas of your life – including money.

Martin Luther said that every Christian goes through three conversions in this order: first the mind, then the heart, and finally the pocketbook. I get it. Learning to trust God with your money is hard. But be encouraged by all the passages in the Bible that encourage you to begin trusting Him with your money. He's going to take care of you and your family. Are you willing to step out and trust Him?

Gratitude

As you begin to think about trusting Him with your money, why not start with gratitude? As we think about what God has done for us, how can it not fill us with gratitude? If you're reading this, most likely you should be one of the most grateful people in the history of the world. Why?

➤ You know how to read.

➢ You were able to get your hands on resources that help you grow in your faith. (Not all in the world can say this, even today.)

➢ Most likely you woke up this morning with food to eat and a shelter over your head. (This may not be true for everyone. One of the most touching stories from the first edition of this book was actually a picture someone showed me. My friend had been at a homeless shelter, and one of the men staying there for the night had a plastic bag with all of his possessions. There were probably a total of twenty possessions. One of those possessions was this book.)

➢ If you're reading this, then you probably already know the love of Christ. Which means someone loved you enough to share the good news of Jesus with you.

➢ Christ died for you while you were still a sinner.

➢ Christ is coming back to spend eternity, face to face with you.

➢ Because I'm only expecting to sell about four of these books (thanks mom and dad), you know me personally, and you probably have an autographed version of this book. How could that not make you grateful?! Kidding!

At least six of the reasons (excluding the last one!) above probably refer to you. Quite frankly, it would not be too difficult to come up with one hundred reasons why we are (or should be) grateful today. When I think of all the reasons in this book of why we should give, and especially when I think about modeling God's generosity, I can't help but want to give generously – out of gratitude. Yes, there are lots of good reasons to give generously. But when I give with a grateful heart, it's like a teleprompter within my mind, telling me that this is a glimpse of heaven. When I give with a grateful heart, it's me embracing, fully enjoying, and being fully alive in God's Kingdom on earth. Gratefulness is a healthy feeling, and it's a healthy reason to give.

To conclude this chapter, let's remember that we have a very generous God. He has given us so much, and it's really our privilege to be able to give. As a Christian do we not desire to take on more of the character of God? Yes, that is our primary aim. So, I'll finish this chapter the way I started it, quoting Ephesians 5:1. *Be imitators of God as dear children.*

Imitator Recap

❖ God is the original giver.

❖ God is a generous God. We should strive to be like God in all areas of life, including being generous.

❖ Throughout the Bible, the tithe, or giving ten percent of all that we earn, is referenced as the benchmark of giving.

❖ The only place where God says *test me* in a positive way is Malachi 3. Here, God is talking about bringing Him the full ten percent of one's income.

❖ God wants us to trust Him with everything, including our money.

❖ We shouldn't give for the reason of receiving. We should give because we love God.

❖ When we are blessed, we ought to pause, and ask, how can I best steward this blessing (whether that blessing be money, a new relationship, another resource, etc.)?

❖ There is perhaps no more powerful reason to give than gratitude.

Imitator Discussion Questions

❖ In this chapter what was the most helpful for you?

❖ Besides the ways listed in this book, in what other ways is God generous? Specifically, how has He been generous towards you? How has He been generous towards all mankind?

❖ How can we model God's generosity?

❖ Why is giving a tithe (ten percent of our income) important?

❖ In what other ways besides financially, can God bless us?

❖ Discuss some of the things that make you most grateful.

❖ Practically speaking, how can we give gratefully?

❖ When we are blessed, why is it important to pause and ask ourselves how we can best steward the increase?

4. **Dalton**

But when you give a feast, invite the poor, the crippled, the lame, the blind, and you will be blessed, because they cannot repay you. For you will be repaid at the resurrection of the just.

-Jesus, *Luke* 14:13-14

It is June 2013. I'm preparing to go on my first *real* mission trip. I stress *real* because I had been on mission trips, but they were typically loosely organized and sometimes ended up being more trip than mission.

After arriving in Kampala, Uganda, I immediately began to fall in love with the people we were meeting. I've never met kinder people than those we met in Uganda. Our church sent nineteen people. We partnered with Compassion International. They coordinated and planned much of the trip. Several people on our team had been to Uganda the year before. One person on our team was actually from there and just met us there. Yes, there was someone part of our church who was from Uganda and just met us there. What can I say, we have a really cool church.

A few months before the trip to Uganda,

Kristin and I began sponsoring a child through Compassion International who lives in the community of the church that we partner with. The child's name is Dalton. The church's name is United Christian Centre.

I will spare you details about the whole trip because I want to quickly get to my point. But all I can tell you, if you ever have a chance to go on a mission trip with Compassion International, do it! If you ever have a chance to support someone going on a mission trip with Compassion, do it! Whether or not you are able to do those two things, one thing you can definitely do is support a child through Compassion. For around $40/month ($38 in 2014) you can provide a lot of the basic necessities for a child.

When we arrived, a part of our trip was actually going to the local Compassion office and seeing the records for our child. I was able to see where my money was going. I saw the child's medical bills that our support went to pay for, education, Bible lessons, food, and a variety of supplies.

One of the first days of our trip, everyone who sponsored a child was taken to the home of their sponsored child. I'll never forget the drive to his house. At this point in the trip we had mostly stayed on the large roads and highways, but for the first time we were getting off the main thoroughfares and taking the back roads. It really felt like I was in a movie. This was the type of scene that you see in the commercials on television where they ask you to support children in poverty.

Granted, this was among the poorest parts of the city, but it was on one hand completely unexpected, on the other hand, exactly what I imagined. It's hard to describe unless you've been there and seen it. Trash everywhere. Standing water everywhere. Children everywhere. Not enough adults. Where are the adults? There are a lot of kids running around.

The roads are almost not existent at this point in our journey. More like dirt paths almost big enough for small passenger cars. Good thing we are in a twenty-two person van.

The homes. What can I say about the homes? The houses were small, and most of them crumbling. There was standing water everywhere. There were mosquitoes everywhere.

We eventually arrived at Dalton's house. I met him, his mother, his sister, and a whole lot of neighborhood kids. We had a translator and he helped us talk for a few minutes. The children's father had left not too long ago. The mother was trying to make ends meet as a hairstylist. I heard from a couple of different Compassion employees that his mother was a very hard worker. After meeting her, I believed them. She had a quiet strength about her. Someone you could tell who had been fighting to live for a long time. The woman embodied fortitude.

The home was roughly ten feet by ten feet. It was clean. It was clean relatively speaking. Almost every part of Kampala we saw was similar in the sense that it was all very dusty and full of dirt. I know calling the town full of dirt doesn't really help to understand what it was like, but to call it dirty wouldn't be right either. It wasn't dirty. But dirt was everywhere. Their home was the same.

There was a couch, a coffee table, a small ten inch or so television that I'm thinking was either black and white or one of the first color televisions. I was later told most of the TVs in people's homes don't work. I'm still trying to verify this. Then there was a bed. The bed was on stilts. Imagine a bunk bed where there was no lower bunk, just the top. That was what their bed looked like. It was either a twin or full size. While only Dalton, his mother, and his sister were home, there were two or three other children at school. It was hard to understand if there were two or three other children living there. It seemed to be complicated, and I didn't push to find out more. Dalton and his sister were not yet old enough for school.

The entire family slept on that top bunk. The reason they slept on that top bunk was because their house was at the bottom of a huge gulch. You wouldn't know it was a gulch just by looking at it. The decline was very subtle, but when it rained, the gulch filled. Sometimes the house would fill as much as three feet or so. It would take a long time for the water to dissipate. There would be days and weeks when their house had several feet of water in it. This happened each year several times.

During one of the last floods, a mother left her children on the top bunk, a set up similar to Dalton's family bed, to go down the street to buy some food for the day. When she returned, her child was floating in the water.

When the translator told me that, the first thing that went through my mind was that poverty would eventually kill Dalton. Though we had just met, and though he never said a word to me, I loved this kid. I loved his whole family. And now I just heard that rain killed a young child just like Dalton.

Dalton was two and a half years old. I had a two year old at home. I couldn't imagine Sophia being forced to stay on the top bunk for days at a time. Without a second parent, of course the mother would eventually have to go out to the market for food. This could have happened to anyone.

If that wasn't enough, they went on to tell me about the sewage. The bathrooms are basically large rectangular buildings with a hole cut out on top. There is a ladder going to the top of the rectangle. When needing to go to the restroom, you climb to the top, do your business and come on down. These things had been built a long time ago. The ones I saw had something that looked like thin sheets of tin to keep the refuse in. The translator told me that they were never cleaned out or emptied. It was very expensive to get someone to come and clean these out. A luxury too far out of reach for the poor. So the refuse just builds up in these things.

Unfortunately, it didn't build up all that much.

It didn't have enough time to build up. Building up would be less worse than the truth. Over time the tin rusted and eroded. The sewage now leaks out. During the floods the sewage is carried into people's homes. Also, to fully paint the picture, it's not like there is only one of these restrooms spilling out refuse. They are everywhere.

As we concluded our time with the family I couldn't get the phrase, "Poverty is going to kill these people" out of my mind. What could I do? I kept remembering the Bible verse Isaiah 6:8 that says, *And I heard the voice of the Lord saying, "Whom shall I send, and who will go for us?" Then I said, "Here am I! Send me."*

God, whatever needs to be done, send me! I began asking around what it takes to get people out of the sewage flood that drowns kids. I was told from a variety of people that I trusted that for $6,000 USD you can buy a home in a safer neighborhood, free from floods.

I knew I had to at least try. Compassion has rules regarding the most you can donate to any particular child in one year. That makes sense. It might not be right for one child to get a house, and one child to get nothing. However, the problem is not that Dalton lacks certain comforts that most in American would consider rights. The problem is that his home may be dangerous enough to merit the special permission. So, anytime there is a special request like this it has to go through the proper channels to determine if Compassion can condone the project.

The Compassion people on the ground in Uganda know what is holistically best for Dalton and his family. I really don't. I've got guesses and I've got opinions, but that's about it. So, I trust their ruling. I don't pretend to understand the complexities of moving a family to another neighborhood. So, I decided to let Compassion run with it and determine if it was best.

Ends up, Compassion believed it was a worthwhile pursuit. In the summer of 2014 we received the green light to move forward on building Dalton a house.

I've learned some very valuable lessons from meeting Dalton. Here are the top ten most valuable lessons I learned:

➤ The money I have today can be used to save lives on earth. It gives me perspective. For every $6,000 I spend over the course of a year(s) on myself with coffees, movies, clothes, whatever, that is one family's lives I could change by getting them into a safer home.

➤ The money I have today can be used to teach people about Jesus. Anytime you give to a church that teaches about Jesus, you are using money to teach people about Jesus. The same is also true with Dalton. The school he will go to (he's currently too young) is a Christian school where he will learn about Jesus. I sat in one of the classes. It's legit. I was with a bunch of eight year olds and I was the one learning new lessons from the Bible. Actually a funny story there. The lesson was on *giving*. And I was taking notes the whole time. I was impressed!

➢ I've been given a lot. Before the trip I would have said I was middle class. Now, I think I live more like a king, relatively speaking.

➢ Access to good medical care is a privilege, not a norm.

➢ You don't have to have money to be happy or nice. Some of the poorest people I met were the happiest and nicest.

➢ Put your hope in God. Those happy and nice people I talked about above were not that way necessarily because they were poor. They were that way because they placed their hope in God alone.

➢ Helping people requires sacrifice most of the time.

➢ Many of the things I do spend my money on seem so lame compared to helping that family get into a safe home.

> My monthly contribution to Dalton through Compassion is probably some of the best $40 a month I spend in any given month. It helps him to get medicine, education, food, and puts him in an environment to learn about Jesus.

> How can I sit comfortably at home, unchanged in my lifestyle, when there are people who a) don't know Jesus, and b) are dying from preventable causes.

This is one of the last chapters that I actually sat down and wrote. I was not positive it would even make it into the final edition of this book. However, in the end I think this chapter is just too important. This chapter is about something I experienced that *validates* everything I've read in the Scriptures about giving, and I haven't been able to forget it since.

By the time you read this book, I have no idea how this story will end. Dalton's old home, in the gulch, is so much more than a shack. It represents a family, that represents a community, that represents in many ways a country that unfortunately represents a large part of the world. So, who knows how the story will end, but I hope we both can take a lesson or two from it.

Dalton Recap

❖ We've been given so much.

❖ There are people who need to hear about Jesus.

❖ There are *lots* of people dying from preventable causes every single day.

❖ You don't have to have money to be happy.

❖ We can use our money to change people's eternity.

❖ We can use our money to help those in need.

Dalton Discussion Questions

❖ If you've ever been on a mission trip, either locally or internationally, have you ever experienced something similar? How was it similar? How was it different?

❖ Yes, it is expensive for someone to go on an international mission trip for one or two weeks, but what are the reasons it's a great idea?

❖ How can we share the Gospel and also help people with their earthly needs?

❖ Has someone ever helped you in a time of need? What was your response to them? What was your response to God?

❖ What do you think of when you compare spending $40 to help a child and his family for a month verses one dinner for two at a restaurant?

❖ Where is the line between balancing wise living and selling all that you have so that you can give it away? For example, should you sell everything you have and spend every last $40 on helping a child in need? Why or why not?

5. **Need**

That light we see is burning in my hall.
How far that little candle throws his beams!
So shines a good deed in a naughty world.

-Shakespeare

Things begin to happen when we give - lots of things. Our faith increases by trusting God with our resources. Our faith can also increase as we receive a front row seat in helping people. For example, when we give, we are able to come into contact with a very real need. We are able to learn more about that particular cause - whether it is supporting an organization or an individual, and our eyes begin to open to new perspectives.

As we give, we are also worshiping God. As we sacrifice to give, it helps us to stay focused on our Savior, who first gave us so much. When we give, we can often be filled with gratitude. As we begin to search for needs that we can help with, we will find that there is *a lot* of need out there. It can fill us with thankfulness that we have most, if not all, of our basic necessities taken care of.

Yes, giving can produce all types of

wonderful fruit in our spiritual lives. But, there is one moving piece specifically that takes place when we give that I want to focus on in this chapter. When we give, we are fulfilling a need. Out of love, we give, and we fulfill real needs.

In God's wisdom He created the world in such a way that He often uses people to help people. There is no doubt that many times God intervenes and miraculously helps an individual or an organization in time of need. But often times, God will use the Church to bring help to those in need. When I say Church here, I'm not talking exclusively about local churches. I'm also talking about those who follow Christ that make up *the* Church. We will talk much more about God using the local church in chapter 14, *How*.

God wants you to trust Him with your money for lots of reasons. One of those reasons is that God wants to use you to fulfill needs here on earth. The Scriptures teach us that God doesn't need us to meet these needs. He can speak the word and the need would be immediately taken care of. However, God wants to use us to help meet needs. That's the way He designed the system to work.

What needs are the Church told to address? Let's look at a number of Biblical passages.

Let the elders who rule well be considered worthy of double honor, especially those who labor in preaching and teaching. For the Scripture says, "You shall not muzzle an ox when it treads out the grain," and, "The laborer deserves his wages" (1 Timothy 5:17-18).

The Bible is clear about the role of Christians to support the clergy (or pastors, priests, preachers, whichever word you use to describe those who do vocational ministry). The main way to support the clergy is to give to the church you attend. You may also know someone serving as a missionary who is responsible for raising their own support. Some clergy are either forced, or prefer, to work a second job to make ends meet. However, it can be very advantageous if the church staff is able to focus on their calling by not having to take a second job.

In addition to supporting the clergy themselves, another need you can meet by giving to your church is by fueling the ministry your church does. What a church can do is limited to the generosity of those who attend it. Your financial giving to your church meets very real needs. Your giving fuels the vision of your church. Supporting those who are called to vocational ministry is one need you are able to take care of by giving.

Another big need you can assist with by giving is taking care of the poor. There are a multitude of verses that talk specifically about giving to the poor. A few of them are listed below:

Whoever is generous to the poor lends to the Lord, and he will repay him for his deed (Proverbs 19:17).

Give to the one who begs from you, and do not refuse the one who would borrow from you (Matthew 5:42).

For I was hungry and you gave me food, I was thirsty and you gave me drink, I was a stranger and you welcomed me, I was naked and you clothed me, I was sick and you visited me, I was in prison and you came to me. Then the righteous will answer him, saying, "Lord, when did we see you hungry and feed you, or thirsty and give you drink? And when did we see you a stranger and welcome you, or naked and clothe you? And when did we see you sick or in prison and visit you" And the King will answer them, "Truly, I say to you, as you did it to one of the least of these my brothers, you did it to me" (Matthew 25:35-40).

One personal note on this verse. I once lived in San Francisco, a city known for its homeless. After consulting with several people who have served in homeless ministries, my wife and I decided that we would not give out cash to people on the street. Several times when we attempted to hand out food, those begging did not want the food. They only wanted cash. Unfortunately, many of them wanted cash for alcohol and drugs. How do I know? They told us.

It's impossible to know who needed cash for survival so they could purchase things such as food or shelter for the night. Furthermore, I felt uncomfortable with my wife opening up her purse and revealing whatever cash or valuables she had in front of - at times - men whose desperation could pose a safety risk.

Our solution was that we would make a special gift to our church's annual offering that went directly to the homeless ministry that the church collectively supports. Now, when someone on the street begs from us, when possible, we explain where the shelter is that we support. There the homeless person would be able to receive incredible services such as food, medical care, life/work training, shower, and clothes.

Here's one note on how to give to the poor - or should I say, one way *not* to give to the poor.

Beware of practicing your righteousness before other people in order to be seen by them, for then you will have no reward from your Father who is in heaven. Thus, when you give to the needy, sound no trumpet before you, as the hypocrites do in the synagogues and in the streets, that they may be praised by others. Truly, I say to you, they have received their reward. But when you give to the needy, do not let your left hand know what your right hand is doing, so that your giving may be in secret. And your Father who sees in secret will reward you (Matthew 6:1-4).

One need that God uses the Church to fulfill is helping other Christians in need. *But if anyone has the world's goods and sees his brother in need, yet closes his heart against him, how does God's love abide in him* (1 John 3:17)?

> *What good is it, my brothers, if someone says he has faith but does not have works? Can that faith save him? If a brother or sister is poorly clothed and lacking in daily food, and one of you says to them, "Go in peace, be warmed and filled," without giving them the things needed for the body, what good is that? So also faith by itself, if it does not have works, is dead* (James 2:14-17).

Deuteronomy 15: 7-11 reads,

> *If among you, one of your brothers should become poor, in any of your towns within your land that the Lord your God is giving you, you shall not harden your heart or shut your hand against your poor brother, but you shall open your hand to him and lend him sufficient for his need, whatever it may be. Take care lest there be an unworthy thought in your heart... and your eye look grudgingly on your poor brother, and you give him nothing, and he cry to the Lord against you, and you be guilty of sin. You shall give to him freely, and your heart shall not be grudging when you give to him, because for this the Lord your God will bless you in all your work and in all that you*

undertake. For there will never cease to be poor in the land. Therefore I command you, "You shall open wide your hand to your brother, to the needy and to the poor, in your land."

This is a great Old Testament passage about how the Israelites were to help their fellow Israelites in times of need. The principle for the Church still stands today.

Furthermore, not only should we help those who work in the ministry, the poor and needy, but also our own family. *But if anyone does not provide for his relatives, and especially for members of his household, he has denied the faith and is worse than an unbeliever.* 1 Timothy 5:8 reminds us that if there is a need among our own family, it's our responsibility to help.

Could you imagine someone who gives away all they have to a great cause, yet neglects his own family? What would that say about his priorities? What would his or her children grow up thinking about their parent's "generosity?"

Giving Leads to Praise

God uses giving to draw glory to Himself. A watching world often has no idea what compels Christians to give. And when people who do not know God see Christians sacrificially giving, it can often spark questions of curiosity. Furthermore, it's not just those who do not know Christ that will be amazed at Christian's giving. I can speak from my own experience that it has been amazing to see the Church support my wife and me in times of need. Note the following verses on God receiving praise as a result of those who follow Christ by giving generously.

...let your light shine before others, so that they may see your good works and give glory to your Father who is in heaven (Matthew 5:16).

...when they speak against you as evildoers, they may see your good deeds and glorify God... (1 Peter 2:12).

You will be enriched in every way to be generous in every way, which through us will produce thanksgiving to God. For the ministry of this service is not only supplying the needs of the saints but is also overflowing in many thanksgivings to God. By their approval of this service, they will glorify God because of your submission that comes from your confession of the gospel of Christ, and the generosity of your contribution for them and for all others...(2 Corinthians 9:11-13).

I'm not sure I know of any more reassuring feeling to have a need met by someone who says, "God has made it clear to me that I'm suppose to give you this." We have a God that knows our every need, and He often uses the Church to fulfill those needs. And when He does, it causes us to worship Him.

I want to conclude this chapter with a verse

that reminds us, that it's not *just* about giving. It's just as much about *why* we give. Our giving needs to be motivated by love. God loves us and He gave his only Son to save us from our sins. It's that love that should motivate us to give. So with that said, as we conclude talking about our opportunity to love by giving, let us not forget 1 Corinthians 13:3, *If I give away all I have, and if I deliver up my body to be burned, but have not love, I gain nothing.*

Need Recap

❖ We should give to help those whose work it is to advance the Gospel, such as clergy and missionaries.

❖ We have a responsibility to help the poor.

❖ Provide for your relatives and especially your immediate family.

❖ We should be generous towards fellow followers of Jesus who have needs.

❖ When we give, it will often cause people to praise God.

❖ If we give away everything, but don't love, we are empty.

Need Discussion Questions

❖ In this chapter what was the most helpful for you?

❖ First and foremost, what should motivate our giving?

❖ How could someone give and not have love? What would be the consequences?

❖ Why is it important to help and provide for those who are in vocational ministry?

❖ What are some practical ways you can help the poor?

❖ Have you ever praised God because of someone else's generosity? What was the situation?

❖ What makes Christian generosity so attractive to people who do not yet believe in Christ?

❖ What would happen if you gave everything to a great cause but your own children lacked even basic necessities? Where - or is - there a line between being generous and asking your family to make serious sacrifices?

5. Need

6. **Riches**

If you have not been trustworthy in handling worldly wealth, who will trust you with true riches?

- Jesus, *Luke* 16:11

We hit the jackpot.

You're reading a book about giving. We've already seen that God is generous, and if that was all, that would be enough. We could fill libraries talking about our generous God, and His invisible attributes like grace, mercy, justice, hope. We could talk about His generosity through His beautiful creation, and we could talk about it endlessly. But, that's not where God's generosity ended.

Immanuel.

God with us. This very generous God we have been talking about has come to earth. He became a man and on earth taught us in human terms what it means to be generous. God has come and He has made it very clear what is expected of us. He taught us how to love God, and how to love others. Jesus taught on many different topics about the way God intended for things to be.

Among the many topics that Jesus taught on, money was one of his favorites. Besides the Kingdom of Heaven, money was the topic Jesus taught on the most. And if I had to sum up everything that Jesus taught us on giving, I would paraphrase *Luke* 16:11 and say, *Go for the true riches!*

True Riches

The passage that has most shaped my perspective on money is Luke 16:1-13:

> *He also said to the disciples, "There was a rich man who had a manager, and charges were brought to him that this man was wasting his possessions. And he called him and said to him, 'What is this that I hear about you? Turn in the account of your management, for you can no longer be manager.' And the manager said to himself, 'What shall I do, since my master is taking the management away from me? I am not strong enough to dig, and I am ashamed to beg. I have decided what to do, so that when I am removed from management, people may receive me into their houses.' So, summoning his master's debtors one by one, he said to the first, 'How much do you owe my*

master?' He said, 'A hundred measures of oil.' He said to him, 'Take your bill, and sit down quickly and write fifty.' Then he said to another, 'And how much do you owe?' He said, 'A hundred measures of wheat.' He said to him, 'Take your bill, and write eighty.' The master commended the dishonest manager for his shrewdness. For the sons of this world are more shrewd in dealing with their own generation than the sons of light. And I tell you, make friends for yourselves by means of unrighteous wealth, so that when it fails they may receive you into the eternal dwellings.

One who is faithful in a very little is also faithful in much, and one who is dishonest in a very little is also dishonest in much. If then you have not been faithful in the unrighteous wealth, who will entrust to you the true riches? And if you have not been faithful in that which is another's, who will give you that which is your own? No servant can serve two masters, for either he will hate the one and love the other, or he will be devoted to the one and despise the other. You cannot serve God and money."

If you were like me after reading that for the first time you are probably asking yourself, "What in the world does that mean for us today?" The dishonest manager of the rich man's possessions was doing a bad job. So, the rich man fires the manager. Then the manager shrewdly calls in two of the accounts he oversaw and hurriedly changes the invoices. He changes the invoices so that the rich man, who was the owner of this business, would never know what these particular customers owed. The only proof of what they actually owed was this invoice. Remember, in those days invoices were not electronically backed-up in the cloud. Now that the invoices were altered, the rich man has no idea how much the customers originally owed. The manager did this so the customers would owe him a favor. Once the manager finally packed his bags for the day and left the rich man's business, it is presumed that the manager would be calling in the favors of the customers he just helped out - perhaps for a place to stay temporarily or maybe for a job.

Now this is where we can start to get confused about this passage. The rich man *commended* the dishonest manager. He saw it was a shrewd move; a move that hurt the rich owner, but a shrewd move nonetheless.

On a much smaller note, I know the feeling. There have been times when I am approached by panhandlers in downtown San Francisco. One line I hear is, "I know where you got those shoes." If you respond with, "Where?" the panhandler will say, "If I tell you, will you give me a dollar?" Now, I've never fallen for this, but I've seen people who have. Once people agree to the terms of the panhandler guessing "where you got those shoes" and you agree to pay the dollar if he guesses correctly, the panhandler will always say, "You got those shoes on your feet."

This is the feeling I imagine the rich ruler having – though worse. He had been scammed, and the elaborate scam of the dishonest manager was at least amusing. Not enough to *not* fire him, but amusing.

The point of this story however, is that people act this shrewd *all* the time. They act shrewdly for things that ultimately do not really matter in the end. True, the dishonest manager didn't want to do physical labor, and he didn't want to beg. However, the dishonest manager probably had other opportunities available. In fact, I'm quite sure of it. The two clients he did "help out," he didn't help them out so much that they would pay his cost of living for the rest of his life. It's an easy assumption that this dishonest manager would later go get another job. In the end, it probably wasn't a life or death situation. And what Jesus is saying here is that we should use this type of shrewdness not for evil - not for ripping people off – but for good; for the sake of telling people about the one thing that can save them.

Be a Strategic Manager

Jesus is teaching us that we need to be *strategic* with the resources that God has given us. Remember when we talked about stewardship in the second chapter? One of the key principles of *good* stewardship is being strategic.

Jesus is saying don't squander your money or use it on useless things. Use it to build God's

Kingdom by resourcing things that teach the good news of Jesus. This is going for the true riches! Jesus is calling us to true riches, and the true riches in this life is having people welcome us into their eternal homes.

It's great to use the money we have to make friends on earth. It's so much better to use our money to make friends who will one day spend eternity with us. That is what Jesus is teaching here. We know from the Scriptures that people will only welcome us into their eternal homes if they are spending eternity with Jesus. We know that people will only spend eternity with Jesus if they hear, understand and accept the good news of Jesus.

So are we using our money on things that help others in someway hear, understand or accept the good news of Jesus? *Let's be good stewards by stewarding what we've been given to help people know Jesus.* That is going for the true riches!

Be a Faithful Manager

The second lesson from the above passage is being faithful in the small things. There was a time when I was a student and I didn't have much of an income. I would give ten percent of it to my church and it would sometimes only be two or three dollars. It almost seemed silly. However, it's what I had, and two dollars was in proportion to the twenty or thirty dollars I was making here and there. Sometimes, it seemed like why even bother taking the time to put this in the offering. Then I read the story of Luke 16 and it corrected my thinking. Jesus didn't care it was only two dollars. Jesus cared that I was trusting Him with what I *did* have.

Some people say, "I make too much to give ten percent. If I made less, then I would give ten percent." No, you wouldn't. As John D. Rockefeller once said, *I never would have been able to tithe the first million dollars I ever made if I had not tithed my first salary, which was $1.50 per week.*

Some people say, "I make too little to give ten percent. I could never live on ninety percent of my income. One day, when I make more money, then I'll give ten percent back to God." No, you won't. This principle is true not only in giving, but in many areas of life, including dieting. Have you ever said, "I will start eating right, later." All of us have either said this or heard our friends say it.

This principle is true with careers as well. Have you ever heard someone say, "Once I'm promoted to a certain position, *then* I will start spending more time with my friends and family." I've seen this principle played out in my personal life and in the lives of my friends. It's confirmed in this passage where God tells us if you are faithful with the little things, you'll be faithful with the big things.

Once you make a decision to do the thing you know you need to do, such as giving, don't wait until your circumstances change. Honestly, your circumstances will probably never be perfect enough to make the leap of faith. When it comes to money, you'll always be tempted to save more. When it comes to dieting, you'll always be tempted to start tomorrow. When it comes to your family, you'll find you always need just a little more time at the office or on your phone. With giving, you'll think that a more ideal time to start is not far off. Don't buy the excuses we feed ourselves.

So, don't put if off any longer. Start now.

Finally, Jesus ends this passage in Luke 16:13 saying you cannot serve both God and money. So true. Have you ever tried to serve both? I have. I tried to save every penny for a house while also trying to give generously to God. I considered both important, and it became a constant tension in my life. I either had guilt that I was saving too little or I had guilt that I was not giving enough. I felt like I would never reach the financial goal I had put on myself to have a certain amount saved up for a house. The result was constant frustration. So what did I do? I had to make priorities in my finances. I decided that the Bible is clear that giving ten percent back to God is the more important thing. For the record, I couldn't find a verse that made me believe becoming a first time home buyer was my top priority.

I decided to return ten percent of my income back to God, before saving anything. I reached my decision to being generous first for two reasons. First, the Bible is clear about the importance of trusting God with our finances. It says that you cannot serve God and money, yet I was trying to do both. If it comes down to serving either God or money, that's an easy one. I always want to err on the side of serving God. Secondly, I knew that at the end of my earthly life, I will be much more interested in how I was able to use my resources to spread the Gospel, and incredibly *uninterested* in how nice of a house I had owned.

Once we are in eternity, our houses and the other material things we spend our money on today will no longer matter. However, people will still matter. I want to leverage my finances now so that more people can hear the saving news of Jesus. If you believe in Jesus, how could you desire anything less than using your money to serve Him?

The Law Of Grace

Let's take a closer look at what giving looks like for Christians today. In the Old Testament, giving seems really clear. You were to give ten percent of your income back to God. There were also special offerings that would happen annually and every three years, but generally speaking, there was the tithe and how much we gave was black and white. Since these Old Testament laws were written specifically for the Israelites, should Christians still follow these rules today – especially in light of the fact that believers today are under grace, and not the law?

One of my favorite pastors and authors, Tim Keller, writes in his book, *Counterfeit Gods*:

> *There have been times when people have come to me as their pastor, and asked about "tithing," giving away a tenth of their annual income. They notice that in the Old Testament there are many clear commands that believers should give away 10 percent. But in the New Testament, specific, quantitative requirements for giving are less prominent. They often asked me, "You don't think that now, in the New Testament, believers are absolutely required to give away ten percent, do you?" I shake my head no, and they give a sigh of relief. But then I quickly add, "I'll tell you why you don't see the tithing requirement laid out clearly in the New Testament. Think. Have we received more of God's revelation, truth, and grace than the Old Testament believers, or less?" Usually there is uncomfortable silence. "Are we more 'debtors to grace' than they were, or less? Did Jesus 'tithe' his life and blood to save us or did He give it all?" Tithing is a minimum standard for Christian believers. We certainly wouldn't want to be in a position of giving away less of our income than those who had so much less of an understanding of what God did to save them.*

Now that Jesus has died for our sins, we are under a covenant of grace, also known as the New Covenant. Some people will say now that Christians are under a covenant of grace, the requirement to give tithes is no longer in effect. Whereas, people who loved God before Jesus were to give ten percent, plus the other required tithes, which would average out around 20%[2] of their income going to God each year. (To be clear, one tithe was to go to the ongoing ministry of the Lord, and one tithe was to go to celebrating God at a feast.)

So, this leads to an important question. Is more, less, or the same required for us today, now that Jesus has died for us, and set us free from the law? To figure this out, let's take a look at other Old Testament laws, and then see how Jesus instructed us to obey them.

During the Sermon on the Mount, Jesus taught through several of the Old Covenant laws such as adultery, anger, and loving your enemies. Jesus says in Matthew 5:21-22:

You have heard that it was said to those of old, "You shall not murder; and whoever murders will be liable to judgment." But I say to you

---

[2] There is some debate in academia whether or not a third mentioned tithe replaced each third year the second tithe, designated for travel to worship the Lord. Regardless, we see the Israelites giving either 20% each year, or perhaps 20% plus an additional 10% every third year.

*that everyone who is angry with his brother
will be liable to judgment.*

Here, Jesus is saying now that we are under the
law of grace, the standard is actually higher. Jesus
says the requirement used to be that you don't
murder, but now Jesus doesn't want us to even
stay angry at each other. Jesus goes on to other
subjects such as adultery and says that the
standard used to be *don't commit adultery*, now
the standard is *don't even have an adulterous
thought*.

With the freedom that the law of grace
brings, it also brings great responsibility. I don't
believe that Jesus was only concerned with this
sampling of topics, but that He intended the
higher standards to apply to all areas of our life,
including money and giving. The standard used
to be ten percent of your giving went to God (not
to mention the additional tithe that went for
traveling to the place of worship, and the tithe
every third year for the needy).

Through Jesus' teaching on the difference
between the Old Covenant and the New
Covenant, we see that today we are not required
to do less, but rather, we have the responsibility
and freedom to do more. Why would it be any
different with our giving? If the Old Covenant
said give ten percent to God, why would we think
today that we should give less?

There are many great reasons why we
should do everything within our control to give
generously (i.e. the reasons in this book). One of

the reasons is because it helps us keep a perspective that God has given us everything that we have. When we give even a small part (ten percent) of it away, that act of returning a portion of it back to God makes all that we have holy, because we honor God with it. The Apostle Paul reminds us in Romans 11:16 that, *If the dough offered as first fruits is holy, so is the whole lump, and if the root is holy, so are the branches.* Since everything we have is God's, God wants us to return a part of it back to Him.

Generally speaking, when we return ten percent of our income back to God, we are being wise stewards. We can know that we are honoring God with the money that He has entrusted to us. Granted, there are things we could do to grossly misuse the other ninety percent that could be displeasing to God. However, as stewards we are given great freedom in how to use the remaining ninety percent, but we must first honor Him with the first ten percent of our income.

Augustine, arguably the most respected Christian theologian who lived in the fourth and fifth centuries, tells us this: *Tithes are required as a matter of debt, and he who has been unwilling to give them has been guilty of robbery. Whosoever, therefore, desires to secure a reward for himself, let him render tithes, and out of the nine parts let him seek to give alms.* I agree with Augustine. We should return the first ten percent of our income, and then use the remaining ninety to continue to be generous.

Should we even call it giving?

I'm cautious in using the term "giving" when talking about the tithe. In the Scriptures, we do not see the idea of us casually deciding to give God our tithes or not. The tithes are simply us trusting God, and *returning* the first portion of what He gave us. In many ways, you can think of it as a test. To illustrate, suppose I give my daughter ten one-dollar bills. I want to teach her to trust me; so, I tell her to hand me the first one-dollar bill back. If she hands it back to me, is she really giving it to me? In the fullest sense, she is actually returning it to me. Besides, I asked for it. Her only decision was to be obedient, or not. By doing so, she is learning to trust me.

If she's wise, she will gladly give the first dollar as I asked. After all, she is getting the better deal here – she gets to keep nine dollars! If she acts selfishly and does not return the first dollar, she would be rightfully concerned about the prospects of me giving her another ten dollars in the future.

For Christians today, I would submit that the tithe (returning ten percent of your income to God) should not be the goal, but rather the starting point. For some, giving ten percent will require faith because the other ninety percent seems so little. For others, giving ten percent will require faith because that ten percent is so much.

Have you ever received a traffic ticket? The police officer hands you the ticket and it's a miracle how much writing they fit onto those little slips of paper. The handwriting is terrible and the whole thing is basically jargon – information that is apparently only understood if you graduated from the Police Academy or your name starts with "Your Honor." But, I don't care about any of that stuff anyways. When I receive that ticket in my sweaty palms, I'm looking for only one thing. How many and how big are the numbers to the left of the decimal place! I have to pay how much!?

If, in your mind, giving and a traffic ticket elicit the same reaction, something went wrong. As good stewards of what God has blessed us with, let's strive for the true riches. Let's not ask how little do we *have* to pay. Let's sit down and ask how much can we give? Giving to things that promote Jesus is great stewardship. Giving is going for the true riches.

Riches Recap

❖ Good stewardship is being strategic with what we've been given to steward.

❖ Be shrewd for things that truly matter – such as spreading the good news of Jesus.

❖ True riches is using our money for things that will cause people to spend eternity with Christ.

❖ Be faithful with your resources - even if it's very little, or a whole lot.

❖ Jesus' grace should spur us to give more, not less, than what was required in Old Testament times.

❖ You have to decide what is your number one priority. It can't be God *and* money.

❖ Don't choose your money over following Jesus. If you do, you'll miss out.

❖ Augustine encourages us to return the first ten percent of our income and to give generously out of the rest.

Riches Discussion Questions

❖ In this chapter what was the most helpful for you?

❖ What are things we can specifically learn about generosity from the act of Jesus coming to earth to save us from our sins?

❖ In Luke 16:1-13, what stands out to you as interesting, confusing, or helpful?

❖ How can we be shrewd with what we have?

❖ How can we use the resources God has blessed us with to go after the true riches?

❖ In what ways have you struggled with living for both God and money?

❖ How should the law of grace lead us to give more generously than those under the Mosaic Law?

❖ What are the implications when deciding to call the tithe *giving* or *returning*?

❖ What are steps you can begin taking today to help you live generously, so that you can go for the true riches?

7. **Blessed**

A blessing is when God gives us something to serve Him with.

– Adi, church planter, Romania

Some people are surprised to hear that the Bible is actually full of promises of rewards for people who trust God with their money. In some ways it seems like if we give while *secretly* wanting a reward, that seems awfully close to giving with strings attached. But if we look at what the Bible actually teaches, it's undeniable that there are great promises for those who give generously. I would even go as far as to submit to you that we should desire those blessings that have been promised. Those desires don't necessarily stem from selfishness, but rather from faith.

Read Mark 10:28-30:

> *Peter began to say to him, "See, we have left everything and followed you." Jesus said, "Truly, I say to you, there is no one who has left house or brothers or sisters or mother or*

father or children or lands, for my sake and for the gospel, who will not receive a hundredfold now in this time, houses and brothers and sisters and mothers and children and lands, with persecutions, and in the age to come eternal life."

Did you know that this passage comes right after the story of the rich young ruler? In that passage, the rich young ruler comes to Jesus and basically says he has kept the Mosaic Law. Jesus tells him to sell all that he has and give it to the poor. Jesus says that if the rich young man does this, he will have treasure in heaven, and then he can come and follow Jesus.

It's easy to forget that Mark 10:28-30 (above) immediately follows that passage. Quite possibly, Peter overheard Jesus talking to the rich young man, and you can imagine that in his mind, he's like, "Wait a minute! I did leave everything behind for Jesus!" Peter tells Jesus that he has given up everything to follow Him. Peter had left behind the family business and his home. What does Jesus say when he hears Peter say this? He says you are going to be blessed in this life and in the life to come.

Basically, because of Peter's sacrifice, he will be rewarded here on earth and in eternity. Not only will he be rewarded, but Jesus tells him he will be rewarded hundredfold - which is ten thousand percent! Not a bad investment. If you want to be a wise steward and give a good return to your Master, then invest in as much as you can in investments that promise a hundredfold return!

What does this look like for us today? Any time we sacrifice for the sake of Jesus and for the Gospel, God is promising that the costs will be outweighed by the benefits. You can invest in these things by giving financially to the local church you attend. You can help the needs of people and let them know you are doing so because of your love for Christ. There are lots of ways you can use your financial resources today to participate in the hundredfold investment.

It's important at this point to talk about what the hundredfold reward is and is not. As Jesus said, that hundredfold can and will take on lots of different shapes and sizes. Yes, you may receive a hundredfold blessing financially. But if you do, it's not usually so you can use that profit to bless yourself. When we look collectively at what the Bible teaches, we see that often God will bless the good stewards because He knows that they will use that blessing on things that promote the Gospel.

So if you begin to give and you miraculously get a raise at work - which may or may not happen – but if it does, don't assume God is giggly wanting you to get a new car. Assume that God is pleased with you being a good steward and that God believes you will also steward this increase well. Find ways to re-invest this increase in things that will promote the Gospel further.

That's not to say that you don't need to use the money on something nice for yourself –

perhaps you actually do need that new car, or a really nice vacation, or even a bigger house. It will take wisdom to decide how you should steward the blessing that God gives you.

With that said, I would add to Adi's quote at the beginning of this chapter that if we don't use what God gives us to serve God, then perhaps it's not a blessing at all.

Perhaps we've turned a potential blessing into a distraction.

When we do receive a blessing from God, let's ask ourselves how we can best steward the blessing. How can we use this blessing to point people to Jesus? I'm not just talking about financial blessing here either. It could be your career, relationships, influence, time, skills, experience, etc. When God blesses us with these things, we have a chance to make a difference. On the other hand, if we consume ourselves with using the blessing on ourselves, what could have been a blessing may actually just be a distraction from the task at hand of pointing people to Jesus.

Jesus says you will receive a hundredfold blessing in houses, brothers, sisters and mothers. He is not saying if you move to a far away country for Christ-centered reasons, and are not able to spend much time with your mother, you'll receive as a blessing one hundred more mothers. He's not saying if you give up one acre of land for the sake of the Gospel that you will automatically receive one hundred acres at some point in this life and in heaven. He's not saying that.

Now those things may happen - they really might. (I'm not sure how someone could have one hundred mothers. Maybe if you were put in charge of a retirement home, that might be like having one hundred mothers? Maybe?) But what Jesus is saying here, and confirmed with what we see from the big picture of the entire Bible, and my own personal experiences, are that when we give up something based upon the reward we receive, our sacrifice will *pale* in comparison. Based upon the reward you will receive in this life and in the life to come, that home on an acre of land will seem like peanuts to the rewards you experience as a result of your sacrifice.

During seminary, when Kristin and I decided to leave our homes and families in the South because we felt God very clearly calling us to San Francisco, we were unsure what our future would hold. Would we be able to afford even the most basic necessitates? Would our homesickness suppress our effectiveness in ministry?

But as we arrived in San Francisco, we *really* began to experience the hundredfold blessing. We had left families, but we were blessed with a strong community. Not long after we moved here, I felt like I had as many friends as I had ever had. Many of these friends even began to feel like family. Furthermore, I've really been shocked at how often my biological family and I get to see each other. Not only have I been pleased with getting to see them several times a year, but our times together now seem sweeter.

While I had fears before we moved that we would rarely get to see each other, those fears were never realized. On multiple occasions someone bought me airline tickets to go see my family back home. Numerous times my family was even able to come out and visit me. Now that several years have passed, my sacrifice of being closer to family has been greatly blessed.

In the same way, I was afraid of leaving the much more affordable South for what would soon be noted as the most expensive place in America to rent. But guess what, God provided for us financially so that we never had a need go unmet.

In the same way, we were blessed when we left our homes in the South. San Francisco apartments are notoriously small. It is depressing to compare the mansions we could afford back in the South for the same price we would have to rent a tiny apartment in San Francisco. Depressing. Have I mentioned that it is depressing? But we've been blessed in huge ways. At this point it would be really hard to convince us to trade in our small condo for a mansion anywhere else.

Back to further defining what that hundredfold blessing really is. Anytime someone writes about giving from a Biblical perspective, you have to include the concept of rewards. You have to do it because there are simply so many Biblical passages on rewards for honoring God with your money. However, anytime someone talks about rewards, you run the risk that the hearer will reason to themselves that they will give simply because they want to try their hand at this whole hundredfold thing. Two things can happen. Some people tend to go into lottery mode. They don't think that if they give, they'll actually be blessed, but why not put ten bucks in the offering plate and see if you don't get a huge payout. Others give, and as days and weeks go by, they never receive a noticeable blessing and they believe the whole giving thing is either wrong or too complicated, and soon give up.

So what's the disconnect?

Many times the blessing must be seen with a godly attitude and perspective. It's only when I look through the lens of the Gospel that I see my small apartment as hundredfold better than a mansion elsewhere. It's only when I look through the lens of the Gospel that I see the community I have now since leaving my old community for the Gospel. I realized that God has allowed me to be part of something bigger than myself by allowing me to be part of pointing people to Him. I realized that all my fears about why I should not sacrifice for the sake of the Gospel were all misplaced; many of them even lies.

There is no doubt in my mind that God has fulfilled the hundredfold blessing promise for me and my family as we packed our bags and moved to San Francisco.

I can't help but to speculate briefly about the future. I obviously have no idea what eternity will look like. I can only imagine what it will look like when I meet people in heaven who I helped in some way share the good news of Jesus. Jesus said the true riches were having people welcome us into their heavenly homes. I can't imagine what that will look like.

But it will have been worth everything.

Think about missionaries who serve in the most difficult locations. Think about certain places in the Middle East where it is illegal to be a Christian. These people have it much more difficult than most of us. Many of them have had to more truly sever ties with their old communities - unable to call or email back home very often for security and financial reasons.

There are people who are living in shacks with no heat or air conditioning in places that get very hot and very cold. There are people who are at times *really* persecuted for their faith. There are people who are jailed, fined, beaten, or even killed for their faith. Have they missed out on the hundredfold blessing? Not by a long shot! These people have none of the material blessings people expect today. But the people I've talked to who have served in these conditions wouldn't have traded it for anything. Why? They possess a Gospel perspective.

They gave up some temporary comforts and luxuries, but they received an incredible amount of joy, faith, love, passion and seeing people follow Jesus. Yes, they had sacrificed every comfort and luxury, but they took hold of the true riches. Once someone experiences the true riches, all other riches suddenly start to look like, well, *false* riches.

Now, let's think back to the conversation at the beginning of this chapter between Jesus and Peter. Put yourself in Peter's sandals for just a moment. Fast forward several years after this conversation that Peter and Jesus just had. Jesus has been crucified and resurrected. There is great persecution for those who claim to follow Jesus and times are hard. Peter is thinking about his family and his old life working the fishing business with his family. He misses them terribly. You can almost see him tossing and turning at night, trying to go to sleep. He has sacrificed everything to follow Jesus. At this very moment would it be wrong for Peter to take comfort in Jesus' promises of receiving the hundredfold reward for what he has sacrificed to follow Jesus?

Of course Peter didn't leave everything behind *just* for the reward. If that were the case, I'm sure he would have given up a long time ago (like that night when Jesus was handed over to be crucified and he denied Jesus three times).

I would like to suggest that it would not be

wrong to take hope in Jesus' promises of blessing, especially when things are unbearably tight. We need reassurance that Christ is going to take care of us. It was an act of faith *believing* that Jesus' promises would come true. Anytime we believe Jesus' words, when those sweet words seem so unlikely to be fulfilled, that is faith. I would submit that the Bible is full of so many promises for people who trust God with their money (or any area of their life for that matter) because God wants to help us overcome the fear of letting go of control.

I picture a father in a pool encouraging his child who is afraid on the side of the pool. The child is too scared to jump in, but the father is saying, "Jump, you're going to love it in here!" But the child cries back, "But it's too cold. It's too deep. I'll never make it." The father, smiling, replies, "It's actually quite warm, it's not too deep, and I'll catch you. Yes, you can make it and once you get in here you're going to love it!"

Our Heavenly Father designed us.

He knows how we tick and He knows what is good for us. But we are often like the scared child on the side of the pool, wanting to come in but too afraid to jump.

As the child, why do I really want to get in the pool? I want to play in the water with my father. But sometimes we need to have specific fears relieved before we make the jump. And just as the father in the pool is trying to comfort his child and tell him all the reasons why he should jump, our Father is telling us all the reasons why we should jump in and trust Him by giving generously.

So once we are ready to do this, what do we *do*? We begin to use the resources at our disposal to go for the true riches. It may require putting some financial goals on hold. When we put our financial goals on hold temporarily, or forever, because we want to go for the true riches, we will be blessed. We can certainly take comfort in knowing that God has promised to take care of us and bless us in this life and in the life to come.

Let's talk briefly about those financial goals that we may need to put on hold. My experience has been that sometimes you will have to make sacrifices in your financial *goals* and sometimes you won't. Many times our financial goals even begin to change as we taste the true riches.

Nonetheless, during most of my life I have been able to budget giving back ten percent of my income to God *without* having to place my other financial goals - such as savings for retirement, college for my kids, etc. - on hold. But without a doubt, some financial goals may not be achieved as fast as you had planned if you are diverting resources from your financial goals to now honoring God with your money. But, let me tell you one thing that I am absolutely sure of - I always want to honor God with my money, even if that means slowing down the pace towards my financial goals.

In conclusion, get a *good* return on your investment. In John 6:27, Jesus tells us, *Do not work for the food that perishes, but for the food that endures to eternal life...* Yes, we can spend everything we earn on food, that which will not last but for a short while. Or, we can leverage as much as we can on the *food that endures to eternal life.*

Which way do you think is better?

Blessed Recap

❖ Get a good return on your investment by investing in things that promote Christ.

❖ When we sacrifice for Jesus, He is going to provide for us.

❖ Jesus says that those who leave houses, family, and lands behind for the sake of the Gospel will receive a hundredfold return in this life and in the life to come.

❖ When you are blessed, assume that you should reinvest the blessing back into things that promote Christ.

❖ The Bible is full of promises of blessing for those who give, in part, so that we will take the leap of faith to trust God with our money.

❖ God takes care of those who trust Him.

Blessed Discussion Questions

❖ In this chapter what was the most helpful for you?

❖ Besides money, in what ways is it possible for God to bless you?

❖ Why do you believe there are so many promises for those who trust God with their money, such as in Mark 10:28-30?

❖ Practically, what did Jesus mean when He said that you could receive a hundredfold blessing? How do you receive a hundredfold blessing of mothers? What might that mean for us today?

❖ How can giving generously cause us to trust God? How can this cause us to grow in our faith?

❖ What about the promises of blessing speaks the loudest to you? Why?

❖ How should you determine how you will use the blessings you receive?

❖ Out of this chapter, what are you most challenged by?

8. **Short**

Once I observed a squirrel crossing a road.
I then realized how short life is.

Most people will live for one hundred years or less - most of us a good bit less. So, let's have a little perspective. Imagine a line that represents eternity. It goes on and on forever. Take one little speck from that line that never ends, and that represents your life. What you do in that little speck - that span of a hundred years or less - can impact that line that never ends; it can impact eternity. Said plainly, what you do in this life affects eternity. Let's explore this idea.

> *Do not lay up for yourselves treasures on earth, where moth and rust destroy and where thieves break in and steal, but lay up for yourselves treasures in heaven, where neither moth nor rust destroys and where thieves do not break in and steal* (Matthew 6:19-20).

According to Jesus' words, where should we store our treasure? In heaven. Continuing, *For the present form of this world is passing away* (1

Corinthians 7:29-31). Why shouldn't we solely focus on earthly matters? Because the present form of this world is passing away. We are only here for a short period of time, then we enter into eternity.

> *Do not love the world or the things in the world. If anyone loves the world, the love of the Father is not in him. For all that is in the world—the desires of the flesh and the desires of the eyes and pride of life—is not from the Father but is from the world. And the world is passing away along with its desires, but whoever does the will of God abides forever* (1 John 2:15-17).

Don't misunderstand this passage. We are supposed to love the world in the sense of loving people and even enjoying creation. The John who wrote this passage is the same John who wrote John 3:16 - *For God so loved the world...* So what does this passage mean for us today? Don't fall in love with the desires of this world because it's so temporary. This passage is even making the point that the earthly things that our flesh and eyes desire will pass away because they are not eternal. These desires are very different from the true riches that Jesus told us to desire. In the passage above, John is helping us to have the perspective that this world is temporary - it's just a blip on the continuum of eternity.

This world is temporary, and Jesus tells us we can actually begin now storing up our treasures in heaven. That sounds like a great idea to me, but how can we do that? Read another parable from Jesus that is found in Luke 12:13-21.

Someone in the crowd said to him, "Teacher, tell my brother to divide the inheritance with me." But he said to him, "Man, who made me a judge or arbitrator over you?" And he said to them, "Take care, and be on your guard against all covetousness, for one's life does not consist in the abundance of his possessions." And he told them a parable, saying, "The land of a rich man produced plentifully, and he thought to himself, 'What shall I do, for I have nowhere to store my crops?' And he said, 'I will do this: I will tear down my barns and build larger ones, and there I will store all my grain and my goods.' And I will say to my soul, 'Soul, you have ample goods laid up for many years; relax, eat, drink, be merry.'" But God said to him, "Fool! This night your soul is required of you, and the things you have prepared, whose will they be?" So is the one who lays up treasure for himself and is not rich toward God.

The rich man in this parable was very wealthy. He had everything he needed. So much so that he had to keep building bigger barns just to store it all. But, and this is a big but, he was not rich towards God, presumably because he hoarded all of his money for himself. He had plenty to be generous with, but he kept it for himself. When he had saved so much, he had to find creative ways just to continue to store it all. And when his time had come and he died here on earth, all his wealth - everything he had lived for - was left behind. Maybe this is where the old cliché, "You can't take it with you when you die," originated.

What this man needed most was what Jesus told us earlier. We must store treasure in heaven. And here's how - be rich in good deeds. Read 1 Timothy 6:18-19. *They are to do good, to be rich in good works, to be generous and ready to share, thus storing up treasure for themselves as a good foundation for the future, so that they may take hold of that which is truly life.*

I love this passage! How are we to store up treasure in heaven? Do good, be rich in good works, be generous and ready to share. And, because this is ultimately a book on giving, I want to highlight *be generous and ready to share.*

By being generous and ready to share, you can do just as Jesus taught us by storing for yourselves treasure in heaven. Paul, the author of this passage, ends the verse with, *that they may take hold of that which is truly life.* Sound familiar? Paul is re-phrasing Jesus' words in Luke 16 when Jesus tells us to go for the true riches.

Therefore, let us be generous and ready to share, so that we can go after the true riches and take hold of that which is truly life. Life here is short, but we can begin today to store treasure in heaven, which is not short; treasures that we don't have to worry about leaving behind; treasures that we can presumably enjoy for that long never-ending line - not just the tiny speck we're currently living in.

Distraction

Matthew 13:22 reads, *As for what was sown among thorns, this is the one who hears the word, but the cares of the world and the deceitfulness of riches choke the word, and it proves unfruitful.* A big part of keeping the perspective that life is short is making sure we don't lose sight of what is most important. In a world with so many distractions, how do we make sure our desire to honor God with our money is not choked out?

Focus.

Are the things that you are doing with your money getting you closer to your goal of honoring God? Are there things you are doing with your money that contradict your goal?

Pay careful attention to the things you spend your resources on. Are they getting you down the field of your goals or not? If they are not, why are you doing them? Are your actions helping you become more of the person that Jesus wants you to be, or are your actions making you become less of the person that Jesus wants you to be?

Some translations of Matthew 13:22 say *the cares of the world.* Others say the *worries of this world.* It's interesting to me that Jesus is warning people that worrying can keep us from being fruitful with our money. In this passage Jesus is even saying that the deceitfulness of riches can keep us from following Him.

Do you ever worry? I do. On the night of my high school prom, I was picking up my date, and when I was opening the door for her, I slipped off a curb and knocked out my front teeth. Since then, I've had quite a journey trying to maintain enough teeth to eat with. Not long ago, I was looking in the mirror, and I saw a small black spot between my two front teeth where I have a bridge. I looked a little closer and I noticed a tiny little hole.

My heart sank. I literally broke out into a cold sweat as I started worrying about how expensive this was going to be. I couldn't stop wondering if it was going to get worse. I couldn't stop worrying about not having time to deal with this. It had me so worried I pretty much spent the rest of the afternoon on the couch stressed out. That evening, I was brushing my teeth. Guess what? It was just a speck of pepper. Again, I wish I could tell you this was 25 years ago when I was a little kid. Nope, I was an adult. A small speck of pepper led to several unproductive hours, all because of worry and the powerful grip it can have. Do not let worry keep you from living the life of generosity that God wants for you.

Not only can we lose focus that life is short by becoming distracted with worry, we can also be distracted by dreams. Are you a dreamer? Dreaming about what the future can be is awesome. But, if all you do is dream, it can distract you just as bad as worrying. Don't let your dreams of striking it rich choke your productiveness. Don't let your incredible work ethic at work distract you from following Jesus. Don't let your desire to rise to the top distract you. Dreaming about what the future can be is a great thing, but don't allow dreaming to lose your focus. Life is short. Don't be distracted by worries, or by excessive dreaming.

I'll end this chapter with one of Epic Church's values. *We leverage what is temporary for the sake of what is eternal.* I love it. We can leverage what we do in this life to affect eternity. By being generous, we can convert our money to the true riches and to take hold of that which is truly life.

Life is short. Stay focused.

Short Recap

❖ Jesus tells us to, *Lay up for yourselves treasures in heaven.*

❖ Be rich towards God by being generous and ready to share.

❖ Most of us will live on earth for less than a hundred years.

❖ What you do in this *very short* life will affect eternity.

❖ Don't allow your worries, or your dreams, distract you from honoring God with your finances.

❖ Let's leverage what we have in this life to go for the true riches and to grasp that which is truly life.

Short Discussion Questions

❖ Contrast and compare saving for the future in this life (like retirement, college, etc.) and Jesus' words to not store treasure on earth.

❖ What are all the reasons why it is a good idea to store our treasures in heaven and not on earth?

❖ What does it mean that the present form of this world is passing away?

❖ How do we love the world in one sense (John 3:16) and not love the world in another sense (1 John 2:15)?

❖ Explain in your own words the parable of the man who built bigger barns for his wealth. What lessons can we learn from this passage?

❖ What are specific ways we can be generous? Specific ways we can be ready to share?

❖ Describe your favorite memory of a time when you shared with someone? How did it make you feel? What was the result? Describe your favorite memory of a time when someone shared with you.

❖ What is *that which is truly life?* What does that actually mean, and what can you do about it?

9. **Scarcity**

No complaint... is more common than that of a scarcity of money.

-Adam Smith

Avoid the mindset of scarcity. It's a great principle I've learned from working with Ben Pilgreen. It's the idea that if you give away something, you will lose that opportunity forever, and it will never be replaced. The Apostle Paul says something similar. *The point is this: whoever sows sparingly will also reap sparingly, and whoever sows bountifully will also reap bountifully* (2 Corinthians 9:6). We see the common theme that those who sow little will also reap little. Likewise, those who sow much, will reap much.

First and foremost, what does it mean to sow and to reap? Sowing is investing. Reaping is receiving your profit (or loss). To continue the agricultural example that Paul started, imagine you are a farmer. You go into your storehouse, and you see your seed. Let's say it's seed for potatoes. Let's assume you have lots of land; so land is not a problem. However, you have a limited amount of potato seeds (honestly, I'm not sure if potatoes even have seeds, but play along). So there you are looking at your seeds. You have them stored in glass jars. As you look at them and contemplate how many of them you are going to sow (or you could use the word, invest), you must decide how many to sow, or to invest, or well, to make things simple, to plant.

Will you decide to plant just a handful? Will you plant ten percent of them? Will you plant half of your seed? Will you plant all of it? Here's the beauty. The more you plant the more you will reap. And what do you reap? You reap potatoes, obviously. And the amount of potatoes you reap is directly in proportion to how many seeds you planted.

This is why Paul used this example. It accurately reflects giving. As you go into your metaphorical barn and look at your metaphorical potato seeds, how much will you invest? You don't have to invest any of it. If you want, you can just sit around and play with your precious little potato seeds all day long, and maybe even snack on a few of them, but wouldn't that be a waste? If you just planted those seeds, they would come out as potatoes – something of *real* value!

An actual potato is worth so much more than just a potato seed. And guess what? The more potatoes you reap, the more seeds you will have to sow.

You simply cannot outgive God.

The more you sow, the more you will reap by which you will have more to sow. I'm so certain of this, that if you've experienced a situation where you are certain you've out-given God, will you put this book down right now and email me at timothy.milner@gmail.com? I would seriously like to hear what happened. For years I've been asking around trying to find a confirmed situation where someone was able to outgive God. I haven't found it yet, and I'm not being sarcastic. I really would like to hear from you.

This idea of planting, reaping a harvest, and then having more to plant is why Paul's example is so beautiful. In the same way today, we can invest our resources into God's Kingdom. The more we invest, the more we will reap, and of course, if we choose, we can just keep all of our seeds to ourselves, but wouldn't that too be a waste?

I've seen a variety of studies, but most say that the average Christian today is giving somewhere between 2-4% of their income. Why do you think the average person sows so little? I believe it's primarily because they lack faith. They believe if they give away what "little" they have, they will have even less. God teaches that this is not the case. Jesus says, *Whoever finds his life will lose it, and whoever loses his life for my sake will find it* (Matthew 10:39). The same is true with being generous. Just like Jesus said you cannot know *true* life until you lose your old life, the same is true with being generous. You cannot know what it's like to be right with God with your finances until you stop living a life of scarcity with your money.

Needed: A New Attitude

Jesus also wants us to have a certain attitude when we give. The apostle Paul wrote, *Each one must give as he has decided in his heart, not reluctantly or under compulsion, for God loves a cheerful giver* (2 Corinthians 9:7). As an executive pastor, it's common for me to talk to people about money. Sometimes when I talk to someone, they may think I'm trying to talk them into giving even though they may have concerns or questions. Nothing could be further from the truth! This verse in 2 Corinthians is what I lean on in these situations. I don't want anyone to give unless he or she has decided in *their* heart to give on their own accord. If you feel pressure or are reluctant, then get to the bottom of why you feel this way. Is it because you've not had a reasonable time to think, plan and pray about giving? Or is it because you lack faith that God will take care of you even as you give? When taking time to develop a plan for giving, take a few days to speak to your spouse (if you have one), pray, and budget. Please, for your own sake, don't think about giving for ten years before you start!

When talking to the Pharisees, Jesus calls the Pharisees out as hypocrites. The Pharisees were great at tithing and following rules, but they were terrible at the more important things, such as justice and loving God. Jesus tells them that they did right to tithe, but they should have tithed while also doing the more important things (Luke 11:42).

The Pharisees were giving, but they were giving in the wrong way. They were guilty of having impure hearts. When they gave, they saw giving as the high cost of being noticed. Even worse, they saw giving as the high cost of making God obligated to serve them. I know what you may be thinking. I would never try to do the right thing so that God would be "obligated" to do what I ask of Him. It's wrong, but unfortunately, it's more common today than you might think. The Pharisees should have seen giving as an investment in God's kingdom, but they presumably, saw giving as a means to be noticed by men and by God.

When we begin to move away from an attitude of scarcity, we will begin to see our money very differently. We'll begin to look for opportunities to invest our resources into God's Kingdom. When we see that giving does not reduce what we have, but rather multiplies it, we begin to see that giving is what ushers in the true riches.

In your heart and mind, decide what you

are to do and go for it. Trust that God will take care of your needs. When you do give, give cheerfully because you can know that you are using your financial leverage to affect eternity. When you buy a TV, the return on that investment will dramatically decrease the 5-10 years you own that TV. When you invest in God's Kingdom, that investment will continue to grow forever - literally forever. Making an investment in God's Kingdom, such as supporting your church, provides the opportunity for others to hear the good news of Jesus. Make investments that matter, and investments that matter will last forever.

The Rich Young Ruler

One of the most well-known, (and can I add, feared?) giving passages in the New Testament is the story of the rich young ruler. He came and asked Jesus what he should do to enter the Kingdom of God (Mark 10:17-27). Jesus tells him to sell all that he has and give it to the poor. Now hang on, I know you may be getting nervous. Don't put the book down yet. Most likely, you don't have to sell all that you have and give to the poor. Maybe that is what you need. But, most of us aren't called to that.

Jesus knew the heart of this young man, and knew that he had made money his god. Jesus knew the only prescription for this man was for him to overcome his money-god by giving it all away. But, what does this story mean to us today?

127

It means don't make money your god. Jesus clearly told this man that all you have to do is give up your money and then follow me. But what did the rich young ruler do? He walked away. He loved his money too much to follow Jesus. What a shame.

The Bible teaches that this life is so short, and after we die we enter eternity. This young ruler hoarded all that he had, and was not willing to let it go, even if it meant not following Jesus. This story asks all of us which will we follow: our money or Jesus?

Do you have enough faith in what God has promised that if you give to Him and to His purposes, then you will be better off? As we discussed earlier, Jesus taught elsewhere that whatever you give up for Jesus you will receive one hundredfold; not only in the life to come, but also in this life (Mark 10:30). I like to imagine that the rich young ruler heard that message before, but the young ruler did not believe Jesus. He decided to trust in the temporary riches he already had.

This could have been a positive story in the Bible. Think about it. Jesus says that you will receive a blessing one hundredfold of what you give, not only in this life but in the life to come. This young man had a lot to give. This man would have received *much* for trusting God with *much*. However, the man decided that Jesus could not be trusted. Instead of the rich young ruler inheriting God's best, someone would later inherit all his wealth and do who knows what with it. What if this story ended differently? What if the rich young ruler did sell all that he had and gave it to the poor? Can you imagine what the Bible would say about that? It would probably be one of those paramount stories like the sinful woman who washed Jesus' feet with her tears. Nonetheless, in this particular story, Jesus was talking to a rich ruler, but He is also talking to us through this story.

If you were the young ruler in this story, what would you have done? Today, if Jesus told you that it was either your money or Him, what would you do? If you're not sure what you would do if you had to choose (which you do), then one of two things is true. You either do not know Jesus as Savior, or you do know Him as your Savior, but you've inadvertently begun to worship a new god – money.

Selfishness

Not too long ago when I taught a small group about money, we covered a wide variety of discussions on the topic. One Thursday evening as our group met, we watched a video from Steve Stroope, pastor of Lake Pointe Church in Rockwall, Texas. Brilliantly, one thing that Steve said was, *When we give, we give away a part of our selfishness.*

When we watched that video we were near the beginning of the group's twelve or so meetings. That night and nearly every future weekly meeting, that quote would come up. It really stuck with me and with several of the members of our group.

I'm not sure how much thought Steve put into that phrase, but those eleven words spoke volumes to each one of us.

His quote reminds me of Hebrews 13:5, *Keep your life free from love of money, and be content with what you have, for he has said, "I will never leave you nor forsake you."*

In a similar note, 1 Timothy 6:10 states, *For the love of money is a root of all kinds of evils. It is through this craving that some have wandered away from the faith and pierced themselves with many pangs.*

In Luke 12:15 Jesus says, *Take care, and be on your guard against all covetousness, for one's life does not consist in the abundance of his possessions.*

If we don't keep our love of money in check, it can begin to rule us. This is probably not a surprise to anyone. Most of us would admit that we've found ourselves making decisions purely on money, or hopes thereof, even if it was against our better judgment. A typical example may be choosing one job because it paid more, even though it kept you from living out some of your other values.

So how do we keep our love of money at bay? We live generously. Each time we give, we are reminded where our true value lies. The best defense a Christian has against greed is generosity. Each time we give, we give away a part of our selfishness.

Why does giving help us to not be selfish? When we begin to think of others and how we can help them in someway, we get our attention off of ourselves. Isn't it intuitive that this is healthy? Don't be selfish. Be generous.

When we live a life of scarcity, we short circuit the life God intended us to live. Too often we believe that if we're going to be able to pay our bills each month, or to one day send our kids to a decent school, or even for our own retirement, we must hoard everything we make. In reality, that is a shame for a lot of reasons. It is so easy for us to think of excuses as to why we can't afford to trust God with our money. For example, we might say, "I can't give money away and pay rent," or "I can't give money away if I want to meet my financial goals." Trusting God takes faith, and living generously starts with trusting God.

God designed our world in such a way that if you truly want to receive, you must first give. God asks for our faith in all areas of our life. Jesus asks, do you believe Me for salvation? Do you believe Me that it is better to forgive than to live a life of resentment? Do you believe Me that you must love your neighbor? Jesus is *also* asking, do you trust Me with your money? Throughout God's grand narrative of human life, He asks us to trust Him in all areas.

Today, will you trust Him with your

finances, or will you continue to live a life of scarcity - never quite having enough to give generously? Though the context is different, we may have more in common with the rich young ruler than we'd like to think. *Jesus' question to us might not be are we willing to give away everything, but rather, are we willing to give away anything?*

Going back to the example at the beginning of this chapter, look into your storehouse of resources, and decide, how much of what you have are you going to invest in God's kingdom - a handful of it, or as much as you possibly can? The choice is yours. Do not forget, however, that what you sow is directly tied to what you reap. So let's sow every seed we possibly can!

Scarcity Recap

❖ Don't fall into a mentality of scarcity.

❖ Living generously begins with relearning that you really can't outgive God.

❖ Sowing is investing. Reaping is your profit.

❖ Make a plan on what you are going to give. Don't give haphazardly.

❖ Don't give to be noticed or to try to get God "on your side."

❖ You are going to sow and reap a little, a lot, or somewhere in between. How much you sow determines how much you will reap.

❖ When we live a life of scarcity, we short circuit the life God intended us to live.

❖ God designed our world in such a way that if you truly want to receive, you must first give.

❖ The best choice is to sow as much as you can.

❖ When we give, we give away a part of our selfishness.

❖ The best defense we have against loving money is generosity.

Scarcity Discussion Questions

❖ Relate Paul's example of reaping and sowing to a story in your own life.

❖ How much seed are you sowing? Is there a way you can take how much seed you are sowing to the next level?

❖ How can you make a giving plan so that you are not giving haphazardly?

❖ Think of a situation where you sowed little. What was the consequence?

❖ Think of a situation where you sowed much. Do you regret it? Why or why not?

❖ Is it possible to outgive God?

❖ In your own words, what does *when we give, we give a way part of our selfishness* mean to you?

❖ What kinds of problem have you witnessed that the love of money can cause?

❖ Can we give and still be lovers of money? If so, what can we do about it?

❖ Is generosity the opposite of greed? Why or why not?

9. Scarcity

10. **Life**

Take hold of that which is truly life.

-Paul, 1 *Timothy* 6:17-18

Does the Bible give us any examples of people who gave the right way? After all, what does it look like to give correctly? There are two key passages that help us understand the big picture of holistic giving. In this chapter I want to explore two New Testament passages that paint a clear picture of what being generous looks like.

So, let's mix things up a bit. In this chapter I want to go through these two passages thought by thought. At different parts of the passage, I'll interject a few thoughts on how we can better understand and apply what we're reading.

While you are reading this, I would ask that you pause after each quote from the Scripture and ask what do you need to do in the next 10 minutes, in the next 10 days, and in the next 10 weeks to get to a place where your life is modeling the example that Paul set for us.

The first passage is 2 Corinthians 9:6-7, 10-13.

6. The point is this: whoever sows sparingly will also reap sparingly, and whoever sows bountifully will also reap bountifully.

If you only invest a little, your reward will be little. Don't let this surprise you. It's a universal law. Let's say you know of a new company that is about to do great things. So, you decide to buy their stock. If you invest $100, your reward is going to be relatively small compared to your reward if you invested $10,000. The same is true in how much we invest into God's Kingdom.

7. Each one must give as he has decided in his heart, not reluctantly or under compulsion,

Give some time thinking about your giving strategy. Don't decide last minute to give more or less than you were planning. For example, while at church if you weren't planning on giving anything that particular Sunday, don't start to panic as the offering bucket is coming your way. Let the bucket pass you by! But, take an opportunity after you get home to seriously think about what God would have you to give next Sunday or whatever your case may be.

For God loves a cheerful giver...

When you give, give cheerfully! Giving is an incredible opportunity for us. Giving should not be compared to getting a traffic ticket, or getting a root canal, or fixing a flat tire on the side of the highway. If the same emotions from those three things pop up when you think about giving, then you are probably not a cheerful giver. (It's okay. I can be that bold at this point. Non-cheerful givers probably gave up several chapters ago.)

10. He who supplies seed to the sower and bread for food will supply and multiply your seed for sowing and increase the harvest of your righteousness.

When you give, God will be pleased. He will likely give you more seed to also sow. In other words, don't be surprised if God blesses you financially so you can increase your giving.

11. You will be enriched in every way to be generous in every way,

If you want to be generous, God will help you be generous in every way. When we want to be like God by being generous, God is going to bless that desire. Once you decide to give generously, expect to find many opportunities to do so!

Which through us will produce thanksgiving to God. 12. For the ministry of this service is not only supplying the needs of the saints but is also overflowing in many thanksgivings to God. 13. By their approval of this service, they will glorify

God... and the generosity of your contribution for them and for all others...

Not only is your giving providing for actual needs, but your giving will cause people to be thankful to God. How great is that? You can use your money to help people praise God.

That is a lot of great information about giving from one passage in the Bible! There is one other passage that has similarities to this passage. But there is one big difference. The following passage is really aimed at people who have money. You could say that the following passage is for the rich. One word of disclaimer before jumping into the passage. If you are reading this, from a global perspective *you are* rich. If today you've enjoyed clean water, plenty to eat, clean clothes and a roof over your head, this passage is speaking directly to you. If you begin to think this passage is only for the millionaires (millionaires who read this, if you think it's only for billionaires) then your view of who this passage is for is too narrow. It is for you!

Let's walk through one more passage from 1 Timothy 6:17-18. Remember, while you are reading this, I would ask that you pause after each quote from the Scripture and ask what do you need to do in the next 10 minutes, in the next 10 days, and in the next 10 weeks to get to a place where your life is modeling the example that Paul set for us.

17. As for the rich in this present age...

Again, if you're reading this, Paul is addressing you; not the billionaires only.

...charge them not to be haughty, nor to set their hopes on the uncertainty of riches,

Do not put your hope in money. It's temporary. You can't take it with you. And quite frankly, it's not as secure as you probably think it is. The economy could tank. You could get very sick. Your roof could need replacing the same month your car dies, which could be also the same month your twin daughters start college. If you put your hope in money, and not in God, there is a very real chance that it will leave you empty in the end.

But on God, who richly provides us with everything to enjoy.

Put your hope in God alone. He alone is worthy of our hope. He is not subjected to the economy, our health bills, or to the unfortunate timing of home repairs or college tuition. Furthermore, God richly provides us with things to enjoy. God will give you enjoyment that your money can't come close to.

18. They are to do good, to be rich in good works, to be generous and ready to share, 19. Thus storing up treasure for themselves as a good foundation for the future,

The rich should be rich in good deeds. They should be generous and ready to share. When we do these things, Paul tells us something very similar to when Jesus told us to store our treasures in heaven.

The good foundation for the future could have two meanings. Being generous will provide a good foundation for this life. If you are generous and always willing to share, and full of good works, you should expect to have a lot of friends. These people will stick by your side in the tough times. Do you know someone like this? If they were to become needy in the future, would you help them? I know generous people just like this, and if I ever learn that they have a need, I would spare no expense in helping them.

The second meaning to this passage is that the future foundation is a heavenly foundation. As the cliché goes, we can pay it forward. By giving, you can store your treasure in heaven.

So that they may take hold of that which is truly life.

Again, Paul is echoing the words of Jesus when He talked about the true riches. Paul is reminding us that if you want to truly live, put your hope in God, give generously, and be full of good works. The opposite would also be true. If you do not give, if you don't serve others, and if you put your hope in money and not God, you will never know what true life is.

Let's put together a giving plan, give cheerfully, and go after that which is truly life!

Life Recap

❖ Sow generously. Don't sow sparingly.

❖ Decide what you will give ahead of time.

❖ Be a cheerful giver.

❖ When you give, expect God to give you more so you can continue to give.

❖ Your giving will cause people to praise God.

❖ Don't set your hope in money. Set your hope only in God.

❖ Be rich in good works, generous, and ready to share.

❖ Your giving lays up a good foundation for the future.

❖ Do all the things above and you'll take hold of that which is truly life.

Life Discussion Questions

❖ How can you sow generously? What would sowing sparingly look like?

❖ What are some practical ways we can avoid giving under compulsion?

❖ Have you thought through what you'll give ahead of time? Why or why not?

❖ What are the practical differences between giving cheerfully and not giving cheerfully?

❖ Why does Paul say God will *multiply your seed for sowing*? What is the purpose behind it?

❖ Why will people praise God because of your giving?

❖ Explain how you can set your hope on God, or on money, but not both.

❖ How can giving lay up a good foundation for the future?

❖ What is Paul referring to when he says go after that which is *truly life*?

11. **Worship**

Worship is giving God the best that He has given you. Be careful what you do with the best you have. Whenever you get a blessing from God, give it back to Him as a love gift.

-Oswald Chambers

Worship is a powerful component of giving. When we sacrifice to give, that is us making a statement that we love God, we love others, and we would rather put their needs above our own. Anytime we put others, including God, ahead of ourselves, we are recognizing that God's ways are best. This is part of worship. There are so many great reasons to give, such as the fact that we are stewards, that we want to imitate God, that Jesus has given us such a clear perspective on what is most important, but one additional and equally important reason to add to the list is worship.

Growing up, I would hear that the act of putting your offering into the plate was the act of worship. I no longer have that conviction. You may still believe that, and I respect that. However, over the last few years, I've come to believe that the act of worship is choosing God's purposes over our own purposes. That is worship. That is how we express our reverence and adoration to God - by choosing Him in all areas of our life, including our money.

If Kristin and I didn't give back to God, we could easily spend that money on a few nice things for ourselves. We could have a nicer car. We could buy a nicer or bigger home. There is probably no limit on the ways we could spend that money on ourselves. However, by acknowledging that God's ways are best, we worship Him by sacrificing in certain areas so that we can give generously. In doing this, we worship Him, and God is pleased.

How do we please God? Hebrews 13:16 tells us, *Do not neglect to do good and to share what you have, for such sacrifices are pleasing to God.*

Paul, in Philippians 4:18 says, *I have received full payment, and more. I am well supplied, having received from Epaphroditus the gifts you sent, a fragrant offering, a sacrifice acceptable and pleasing to God.* Again, a different author of the New Testament letting us know that giving is pleasing to God.

When we give generously, God is pleased with the sacrifice. It's incredible that by making specific decisions on how we use our money, such as deciding to give, we can actually *please* God. That sounds like a good thing to do!

The Macedonians were poor. Very poor. Yet they gave, and they gave generously. See Paul's words,

We want you to know, brothers, about the grace of God that has been given among the churches of Macedonia, for in a severe test of affliction, their abundance of joy and their extreme poverty have overflowed in a wealth of generosity on their part. For they gave according to their means, as I can testify, and beyond their means, of their own accord, begging us earnestly for the favor of taking part in the relief of the saints— and this, not as we expected, but they gave themselves first to the Lord and then by the will of God to us. Accordingly, we urged Titus that as he had started, so he should complete among you this act of grace. But as you excel in everything—in faith, in speech, in knowledge, in all earnestness, and in our love for you—see that you excel in this act of grace also (2 Corinthians 8:1-7).

This is a great example for each of us to strive to be like! There are a few key takeaways from this passage. The Macedonians didn't have a lot of money, but they gave generously. Each gave according to what they made, but they also gave beyond their means. In other words, we could say they each gave a certain percentage of their income. Of course, the actual amount would be more for those who had more, and less for those who had less, but they each sacrificed equally.

They gave more than what would *ever* have been expected of them. They eagerly wanted to give! Reading between the lines, you could see that because Paul saw their poverty, he may have been reluctant to take such an offering from them. However, the Macedonians begged him to take it! Paul is telling the Corinthian church about the Macedonians, and tells them to also excel in faith, speech, knowledge, love, but to *also* excel in the grace of giving (verse 7).

The Macedonians worshipped God with their money by giving generously. They did not know at the time, but two thousand years later, we would still be hearing the example of their generosity. We would still be glorifying God because of their gifts.

Perhaps there is no clearer example of worship through giving than the story of the wise men when they visited the baby Jesus. Matthew 2:11-12 says, *And going into the house they saw the child with Mary his mother, and they fell down and worshiped him. Then, opening their treasures, they offered him gifts, gold and frankincense and myrrh.* The wise men, when arriving at the house where Jesus was, fell down, worshipped, and gave Him gifts.

If you were to arrive at the house of baby Jesus, would you bring a gift? Would you bring just something you had laying around the house - something you were looking to get rid of anyways, or would you bring Him your best? Let us worship Jesus by giving generously.

Worship Recap

❖ Worship is an important component in why we give.

❖ Anytime we put God's will above our own wants and desires, we worship Him.

❖ We express our reverence and adoration to God by choosing Him in all areas of our life, including our money.

❖ Giving pleases God.

❖ The Macedonians gave beyond their means and even begged Paul to let them give. Paul tells us to be like the Macedonians in the grace of giving.

❖ The wise men came to Jesus, worshipped, and gave Him gifts.

Worship Discussion Questions

❖ In this chapter what was the most helpful for you?

❖ What is worship? How can we worship by giving?

❖ Is sacrificing the same as worship? Why, or why not?

❖ Why is God pleased when we give?

❖ In what ways are you similar to the Macedonians? Different?

❖ What is the most important lesson from the Macedonians that you need to apply to your own life?

❖ How can you be like the wise men by worshipping and giving?

12. **Faith**

As your faith is strengthened you will find there is no longer the need to have a sense of control, that things will flow as they will, and that you will flow with them, to your great delight and benefit.

-Emmanuel Teney

Ever since I was young and still receiving an allowance from my parents, I have given ten percent of what I earned to the local church that I attended. My parents taught me the Biblical principles of giving from an early age, so it was only natural that I grew up doing the same. When my wife, Kristin, and I began seriously dating we talked about giving and it was always certain that once we were married, we would continue to give ten percent of our income to our church.

During the first few years of our marriage, Kristin and I were giving ten percent of income *after* taxes were taken out. Eventually, this got to a point where faith was no longer needed. Giving the ten percent became routine. As we gave, we were given more to steward, and it did not require faith to continue giving the amount we were giving.

Kristin and I decided we would start tithing on our *gross* salary (that is the amount before taxes are taken out). We began to stretch our faith in our giving again. God even provided us with additional income. The book of *Luke* states that if you are faithful in the little things, you will be faithful in the big things as well (Luke 16:10). I have seen this principle play out, and I can share with you from my personal experience that as I have given more, God has given me more to give. Please note that I'm not saying that if you give God ten dollars, He is going to give you a thousand dollars within seven days or your money back.

God is not a slot machine. God is not a lottery.

I don't presume to tell you how God will provide for you. However, as we've already seen, Jesus does tell us, *Everyone that has left houses, or brethren, or sisters, or father, or mother, or children, or lands, for my name's sake, shall receive a hundredfold, and shall inherit eternal life* (Matthew 19:29). This is significant. We will be rewarded in this life. And we will be rewarded in the life to come. On the one hand, we will receive blessing in this life. Though keep in mind the blessings of this life will be relatively short lived. On the other hand, we receive treasure that will last forever in heaven. Jesus tells us, *Lay up for yourselves treasures in heaven, where neither moth nor rust destroys and where thieves do not break in and steal* (Matthew 6:20).

What makes these Scriptures so exciting to me is that it's not a charlatan on TV making these promises; this is *Jesus*. If you trust Him with your soul, why wouldn't you trust Him with your finances?

When Kristin and I moved to San Francisco to be part of the team to start Epic Church, we decided that we wanted to test the notion that you can't outgive God. Though our budget was very tight, we decided we wanted to increase our giving by one percent of our income each year. Only a few short months after we increased our giving to eleven percent, Kristin was offered a new job making more than her previous job. Since we had a little extra money at the end of the month, we decided we would give even more to our church. Shortly thereafter, Kristin got another job making even more than the previous job. Not only were we given additional income to steward, but Kristin loved the job, which was perhaps the biggest blessing. Now, you or I, or anyone, could say these two instances were just coincidences.

However, I am unable to accept that as the case. We decided to increase our giving to further invest our money into God's Kingdom. When we did, God provided additional resources to invest. You can say it was just luck and the timing of the new jobs simply had *interesting* timing. However,

I believe it would take more faith to believe that than to believe God fulfilled His promise to take care of us. I also believe that as we were looking for ways to be more generous, God provided additional resources for us to be generous with.

Beginning to give *anything* to God is a challenge. It takes faith. When we moved to San Francisco, we were paying almost six hundred percent more for our rent for approximately the same sized apartment in New Orleans. Our living expenses were huge compared to what we were used to, and at the end of the month we had nothing left over. Being the planner that I am, I could see that if we gave more to God, we would be going into savings by the end of the month because our budget was so tight. If God didn't provide for us soon, we would quickly find ourselves in a difficult situation.

If I didn't believe that God would provide for us as we gave, I would have stopped giving or at least reduced our giving. There were plenty of walks around our apartment complex as I would pray out to God, "You're sure I am suppose to give ten percent, right?" Or, "God, the numbers aren't adding up. What am I suppose to do?"

If the benefits of giving sound too good to be true, in one sense you are right. It's not that easy. There will be times when you question yourself if indeed you are giving generously. If you have close friends or family who know about your generous giving, sometimes they will even question your sanity. There have been times when we have been tempted to lower our giving and instead of trusting God with our finances, we have been tempted to trust what we had at Wells Fargo.

After years of giving, I have learned that many times the temptation to stop giving is the strongest right before God provides for a need. Through these trials we have learned to lean on God in times of doubt and uncertainty in areas of our finances. When we began to regularly give eleven percent of our income, my mind was full of self-doubt. I wondered if maybe I should be putting that money in a savings account so that we could have a down payment on a house of our own one day. Or maybe we should spend that money on travel. I mean, if we live this close to Hawaii, surely it's God's will that we vacation there, right!? However, we stayed strong and continued to give.

A few months after we increased our giving, we got word that Kristin received a pay increase at work. Not only was God continuing to bless us by providing for our needs as we continued to give more, but our joy and happiness increased as we were able to give more and more to things that mattered to us and to God. Now, giving eleven percent didn't seem so challenging. So guess what? It was time to stretch our faith once again.

Trusting God with anything, including your finances, is difficult. However, the benefits of doing so are truly priceless. God giving us the extra income was nothing compared to seeing God provide supernaturally, *in a natural way*, at

Kristin's work to provide for our needs. You can take all the money away from us and set it on fire, but you can never take away the joy Kristin and I had after we saw God provide for us.

Comfort in Money is a Bad Idea

In the book of Job, we see that God taught Job to find comfort in Him alone. Before Job went through hell on earth, he had everything you could ever want, and it's conceivable he became comfortable. Not comfortable in a bad way, but in a way that is only natural. It's simply human nature to feel comfortable when we don't perceive any needs.

Then one day, it was all taken away from Job for a period of time, and he learned to take comfort not in riches, but in God alone (and quite frankly that was all he had).

We do not give to receive, but when you give you will realize that God giving you additional resources is only the beginning. God's greatest blessing through this is shaping us into people who take comfort in Him alone.

As Kristin and I keep giving, I pray that God will continue to give us more and more so that we can turn around and be a blessing to our church and our community.

Money is ultimately a tool. We must use the tools Jesus has given us - money, time, talent, etc. - to further His Kingdom. John Piper once said at a *Passion* conference that, *God doesn't bless you to be a cul-de-sac of His blessing. He blesses you so that you can be a conduit of His blessing.*

By no means should you never spend money on yourself. I see how I spend my money on a continuum. On one end of the line is spending my money on me. On the other end of the line is spending my money on others. Most people, Kristin and I included, have to spend most of our money just to pay our bills. However, there is a portion of our money that we have discretion on how we spend it.

With that said, I'll even go as far to say that giving should be so important to everyone who follows Jesus that we would be willing to make sacrifices in order to give. I don't give because I have a little left over at the end of the month. I give first, and then find ways to live on what I have left.

When I do have extra resources, I get to decide how to steward that money. Every time I spend money on things that I *want* but don't necessarily need, such as a movie, it shifts the needle a little to the *me* side. When I give additional money back to God, I shift the needle towards the *others* side. I want to organize my family's finances in such a way that we are able to keep moving the needle to the *others* side as much as possible. Kristin and I would both agree that many times we have to spend the money on ourselves. Date nights for Kristin and I are not in the want column. They are in the need column. I need to spend one on one time with my wife. Forsaking going on dates and splurging on my wife wouldn't be doing anybody a favor. From time to time we must be able to relax.

Eating out every meal is not in the *need* column. We would both agree that when we are able to give more to God than we had originally planned, it is infinitely more exciting and valuable than a couple of steaks at a restaurant.

Being the executive pastor at Epic Church, one of my main responsibilities is the finances of the church. I hear story after story of people who tell me how God has come through in some way and that you cannot outgive God. We have a generous God who wants nothing more than for us to be generous as He is. My life, and the life of Kristin, is a living testimony that giving is a key way to grow your faith. I pray that you will take the next step in faith and learn first hand that you cannot outgive God. More importantly, my hope for you is to find the joy that giving creates in your life as you increase your faith, obedience and your love, as you see others come to know Jesus.

Faith Recap

❖ Tithing has challenged and grown my faith. It has helped me to trust God not only with my money, but in all other areas of my life as well.

❖ Every time Kristin and I have decided to give more, God has provided for us so that we could give more.

❖ Giving generously takes faith. It is not always easy. It is always rewarding.

❖ Seeing God prove Himself faithful to the promises He has given us in the Bible has been priceless for Kristin and myself.

Faith Discussion Questions

❖ In this chapter what was the most helpful for you?

❖ Why does God bless us when we give?

❖ What should we do if and when God does increase our financial capacity?

❖ Describe a time when you went out in faith (in any area of your life). Are you glad you did it? Do you have any regrets from doing it God's way?

❖ If you were honest, which do you prefer, financial blessing or seeing God provide? Why?

❖ Many times we want God to bless us in such a way that financially we no longer need to rely on Him. Is this a healthy desire on our end?

13: **Legacy**

When I stand before God at the end of my life, I would hope that I would not have a single bit of talent left, and could say, "I used everything you gave me."

-Erma Bombeck

There is a man named Robert. He and his wife, Lou, are very generous. They often sacrifice so that they can provide for the needs of others. They know that what really matters in this life is that people know Jesus. They are not so concerned with having the nicest house on the block or having the most luxurious car in their driveway. They use their money to help others, to support the ministry of their church, and give to causes that teach about Jesus all around the world. Both Robert and Lou will leave a legacy of generosity to their family, church and community because they are faithful with what they are entrusted with.

Robert and Lou have a son named Tom. Tom grew up learning from his parents generosity. As Tom grew up, so did his generosity. Tom now gives well past the point of sacrifice - to the point where his lifestyle leaves the fingerprints of generosity everywhere he goes. Tom lives well beneath his means for one reason: so that he can give more. Tom knows that the most important thing in this world is to teach people about Jesus. To that end, Tom has dedicated his life to giving as much as he can in order to point more and more people towards Jesus.

Both Robert and his son, Tom, will leave legacies of being generous with what they have. They will also leave legacies of believing in God and trusting Him with their finances. Both Robert and Tom have an incredible faith that the Bible is full of God's promises for those who trust Him with their money.

Tom has a son - me.

I have grown up learning the importance of being generous from my dad and grandparents. I not only learned these things from my dad, but I also see the joy that my father has when he gives. I see that many people spend their money on things that over time will stop providing happiness for them.

Many people receive their joy from either things that will eventually break down, must have the roof replaced every twenty years, or things that can be scratched and torn. This contrasts strongly with the never ending joy my dad has. Not only have I now seen the joy that giving has given me, but over the years I have seen how my family has been impacted by a legacy of generous givers. This legacy of givers, including my father, his father, and many others in our family, has greatly impacted the lives of my wife, daughters, and me. They have also impacted our communities, and even the far reaching corners of the world.

In *Why We Give*, I come to you as someone who has been deeply touched by generous people.

People who are leaving legacies.

I have seen the promises God makes towards the generous put to the test, and proven true many times over. So what does God promise about being generous with your money? Money is one of the most talked about subjects throughout the Bible - in both the Old and New Testament. Jesus talks more about money than He does heaven and hell combined. Jesus talks about money so much because He knows that your money is directly connected to your heart (Matthew 6:19-21).

If you want to know what your heart is connected to, take a look at your last bank statement. You spend your money on the things you value the most. If you love to look good, you're going to see you bought a lot of clothes. If you love to be entertained, you're going to see you spent a lot on entertainment. If you love knowledge and learning, you'll probably see you bought a lot of books. But what does it mean when you look at your bank statement and you gave nothing or very little of what you made to God? Seriously, what does that mean? Does it even matter?

I meet people every week who love Jesus. They follow Jesus. Many of them are active in spiritual disciplines such as daily Bible reading, volunteering, praying, journaling, and small groups. These people are following Jesus by loving God and loving their neighbors. However, I am finding that too many people who love Jesus have no idea what He teaches on giving and money. I wrote this book to plead with you to see what the Bible teaches about giving. *Through this book I have tried to make the strongest case I can on why you should give back financially to God.*

If you've had your life changed by following Jesus, you know how incredible it is to finally have peace in your life and relationships. Maybe you lived a life of despair, never understanding what life is all about. But after having your life changed by Jesus, you experience joy for the first time in your life. It isn't temporary, and yes there will be ups and downs, but it is a joy that never goes away.

Maybe you know someone who never got along with anyone. People hated them and the hate was mutual. But then Jesus changed their life. Now, they have healthy relationships. These dramatic life changes are also suppose to happen in the area of your finances. Too many people who love Jesus walk around completely unchanged in the area of their finances. Their finances look exactly how they did before they met Jesus.

This isn't right.

Some of the most stingy and selfish people I know pride themselves on being generous. They may give a few dollars here or there, but it in no way changes their heart because their small gift requires no thought, sacrifice, or faith.

I want the truths found within the Bible to force us to be honest when we ask ourselves, "Am I a generous person?" I want to submit to you that the Bible is very clear on how we can honor God with our money.

People today believe that if you want to be wise, you have to hoard. I know, because I lived a lot of my life like that. What I have found is that the opposite is actually true. If you want to truly be wise and to honor God with your finances, you must be generous.

Join me in being intellectually honest with ourselves and with God as we explore what God wants for us in the area of our finances. Let's put our preconceived ideas about what we think about the Bible and money on hold, if just for a moment, and take an honest look at what God has taught us about money. We all know that if

God has told us to do something, *anything*, it will always be in our best interests to do it His way. If you're anything like me, you know the pain you can cause yourself when you go against the grain of God's will for your life.

I want to wrap up this chapter with a story. It was a weekday afternoon. I was sitting in my office with two people that I work with. We were having an impromptu meeting, discussing some business of the church. At one point as we were chatting, an unknown man walks right into my office. My desk was off to a corner and he had not seen us immediately. The moment he saw us, he said he was looking for an office on this floor, and thought that perhaps my office was the one he was looking for. It wasn't. Or well, that is what he said. We told him who we were and pointed him to the directory in the lobby where he could find who he was looking for.

The moment he walked out of the office, alarm signals were blazing in my head. This whole man's act was suspicious. Why was he here? Why did he walk so confidently into my office if he was not positive where he was going? But I didn't say anything. I was too embarrassed to say anything. I reasoned that it was nothing and that he truly was an honest guy just looking for some other office. So I let it go.

We finished our meeting a few minutes later. The others who were part of the meeting went off to their separate offices down the hall. A couple of minutes later one of my coworkers briskly walked back into my office and they didn't have to say a word. I could easily read the expression on their face. Their office had been robbed. I went looking for the guy, and I wish I could have told you that I found him and got the computer back that he stole. But I didn't. Never found him.

From that moment forward, I vowed that if I ever felt strongly about something, I would at the *least* voice my concern to hopefully avoid something preventable like this break-in from happening again.

That is why I wrote this book. Those who follow Jesus and are not yet trusting God with their financial resources are missing out on something huge. You're missing out on leaving a legacy.

A legacy of pointing people to Jesus.

Throughout this book I've tried to get your attention to the fact that giving is an extremely important part of a Christian's life. What you decide to do with the knowledge is up to you. But in order that I can sleep at night, I have to tell you why we give. I pray it leads you to give generously and sacrificially. And if you do, you and God's Kingdom will never be the same.

Legacy Recap

❖ You can use the resources you've been entrusted with to leave a legacy of pointing people to Jesus.

❖ Leave the fingerprints of generosity everywhere you go.

❖ When we seek to become more like Jesus, we must learn to be generous as He is.

❖ If you want to know where your heart is, look at the transactions in your bank account.

❖ Jesus talked more about money than almost any other subject because He knew that where your treasure is, there your heart will be also.

❖ Giving is an extremely important part of a Christian's life.

Legacy Discussion Questions

❖ How can you leave the fingerprints of generosity everywhere you go?

❖ How can you specifically become more like Jesus in the area of generosity?

❖ What does it mean if you look at your bank account and see that you gave very little of your income towards things that promote Jesus?

❖ What do you think Jesus meant when He said that where your treasure is, there your heart will be also? Because of this fact, what do you need to do?

❖ Why is leaving a legacy of pointing people to Jesus a good reason to give?

14. **How**

I know what to do. I know why to do it. But I have no idea how to do it.

As a smart person, there is no doubt in my mind that with enough time, effort, prayer, Bible study, focus and concentration, you could figure out exactly *how* to give. However, I would like to save you some heartache and time. I've had a lot of time to think through some of the most common questions I hear about how to give, and I would like to share with you my conclusions. I believe you will find it helpful. Whether you are just beginning to *think* about giving, or you have been giving your whole life, you probably have questions yourself. Even if you don't think you have a question, I would really like you to read this chapter. After reading the questions and answers that follow, I believe you will learn a few things that can help you better honor God with the money He has entrusted to you. In this chapter, I have listed out and answered the most commonly asked questions I have received.

Should I give the ten percent of my income to my local church?

One of the most common questions I get from people who are interested in giving is where should they give. Today, there are lots of places to give. You can give to your church, to other ministries in your community and around the world. There are also a plethora of nonprofit organizations that are doing good in your community.

So, with so many choices as to where you could give, what should we do? What does the Bible say about this? The Old Testament was written at a time where there was practically only one place you could possibly give – the Temple (or Tabernacle before the Temple was built) or your local synagogue. In the New Testament it's reported that people brought their gifts directly to the Apostles, which was likely wherever that group of Christians met regularly, such as in a person's house.

Today, however, with technology and easier forms of transportation, it is possible for people to be part of many different ministries. For example, you may want to support your local church, support other great ministries, such as Compassion International, and ministries that support your local community. For people who want to honor God with their money and give, what should they do?

The advice I give is this. I always give my ten percent tithe to the church I attend. If I want to support other ministries, I do that in addition to my tithe. If you believe in the church you go to enough to go there, you should support it financially. You need to believe in the vision of the church you attend. You need to be a part of a church that you can support wholeheartedly.

If you don't care or trust your church to support it financially, you need to find a church you love enough that you can also financially support. Let's say you are so passionate about orphans that you would rather give money to orphans than to the church you attend. Find a church that is also passionate and active in supporting orphans, or support your favorite ministries to orphans with money that is above and beyond your tithe.

The reason I advise this is because I believe there is no organization more important to advancing God's kingdom holistically than the local church. Let's think for just one moment what a typical church does.

➢ *Every* week there is the proclaiming of the Gospel of Christ. For 20-60 minutes the speaker/pastor has everyone's undivided attention and is able to speak God's truth to their lives.

➢ There is a time of worship through live music every single week.

➢ There are opportunities for the church to be the Church by serving on Sundays, (or whenever your church has services) and during the week.

> The church organizes and facilitates local and foreign mission work.

> It provides a means for going deeper in one's faith through Bible studies that break people into small groups.

> It provides a way to care for those who come; if you find yourself in need one day, who are you going to reach out to first? Many of you will say your church, or at least, people from your church.

> It's where your community of friends are. Think of the people you trust the most. How many of them do you know from the church you attend?

> The church provides structured, intentional, and age appropriate learning activities for your children.

> The church provides organized efforts to reach people in the community who do not know Jesus.

> The church performs baptisms and communion.

> ➤ Many people are married in their church or at least by their minister.

> ➤ Many people dedicate their children in their church.

> ➤ Many funerals are performed by a minister from their church.

> ➤ If you have a spiritual question, who can you ask? Staff or leaders at your church.

> ➤ If you meet a neighbor, and they want to follow Jesus, what are you going to invite them to do? Will you invite them to come along to your church?

> ➤ Related specifically to giving, the church is set up and equipped to handle resources responsibly.

Basically what I'm trying to say here is that the local church is tasked and equipped to spread the Gospel. There are lots of great places to give, but I can't think of a single organization that can come close to the effectiveness of spreading the Gospel and discipling people like the local church. That is why I give first to my church. I give ten percent of my income to my local church. Things that I want to support outside of my local church, I give beyond my tithe.

And yes, there are causes that my wife and I do support outside our church. There are incredible ministries out there. However, as a steward, I believe the most strategic place I can invest the money God has given me to manage is my local church.

As mentioned earlier, if the church you are part of honestly doesn't do some of the important things mentioned above, you need to ask yourself, is that where you belong? However - and this is a huge however - if you've found yourself getting involved in several different churches in the last year because none of them satisfied your needs, desires, opinions of what a church looks like, the problem could be your expectations. As much as I like to talk about how important the local church is, please understand there are no perfect churches.

Sometimes the church we go to is actually the problem. Many times it's our attitude or perspective. Seek wisdom on this. If you're not sure about the church you go to, call up a Christian friend that you have in another state or city. Explain the situation and ask them to truthfully tell you if you need to find another church, or if you need to stick it out where you are. Again, there are no perfect churches out there. And when I say call someone up, I don't mean gossip. Don't start asking people in your church why pastor so-and-so doesn't ever do this or that. That is not helpful and will unnecessarily cause division.

I dream of a day when the local church will have the resources it needs to fulfill the vision God has for it. The ministry your church does is a direct result of the giving of those who attend your church. As giving increases, additional ministry can be done. As giving decreases, the amount of ministry goes down. Churches are rarely ever funded by anything other than those who come to the church.

No church ever has a money problem, only a faithfulness problem. The people who attend any given church have the resources to fuel the ministry of that church. All that is needed is for the people to be generous with what God has given them in the first place. Begin to give generously to your church, so that it can do the work that it is called to.

From my experience in working at a church, can I give a couple pieces of inside information? First, automate your giving. If giving is important to you, set up your gift so that it is automatically sent on the dates you choose. This might sound crazy, but when a church has low attendance because of holidays or weather, it almost always results in the giving being much lower. This can, of course, make it difficult for the church to stay on budget. This problem is overcome by automated giving.

The most cost effective way to give to your church at the time of writing this is either a) using the Bill Pay feature of your bank to send a check to your church or b) using ACH giving found on many church's online giving websites. Both of these options are attractive because it means more of your money is able to go to ministry and less goes to transaction fees. The typical credit card transaction fee is around three percent. ACH is typically around fifty cents per transaction regardless of the amount. Bill Pay is completely free to you and to the church.

In closing on where you should give your tithe (remember, tithe is ten percent of your income), I'll leave you with a quote that shines light from a historical perspective of the early Church. Wayne Jackson, of the Christian Courier writes:

> *The notion that one may simply free-lance his contribution in doing good, with no obligation to the local church, is a myth contrived by the covetous. Wherever else the saint may give, his weekly contribution to the local congregation should be unwavering.*

What do you do if your spouse is not on board with giving, but you feel God leading you to give?

Is your husband a Christian, yet he is just nervous about giving? Ask him if he would take the Three Month Tithing Challenge (See chapter 15, *Vanity*). Is your wife a Christian, but giving is just a new topic to her? Sit down and read with her where the Bible talks about giving and money. Use the appendix in the back of this book to walk through various Biblical passages on giving. If these solutions are not appropriate, and you are unable to agree on giving, I recommend that you tithe on the income *you* make.

Don't expect a non-Christian to want to support God with his or her money. But, you can be a living testimony to your spouse by tithing what you make. Let's say your husband knows you want new clothes, yet you have decided to put that desire to the side temporarily, so that you can tithe this month. It's a powerful example when your husband sees that it is more important for you to give to God than to buy new clothes.

Maybe you're a stay-at-home mom, and you don't have an income. When you do earn income or receive a financial gift, tithe it, even if it's infrequent or not very much. Recall the story of the widow who gave all she had which was the modern equivalent of less than a penny. As Jesus saw her give this gift, He said she gave more than the people who were giving large gifts because she gave all that she had (Luke 21:1-4). Let your giving, no matter the size, serve as a sign of your faith. And no matter what the reason is for your spouse not wanting to give, you can pray for them. Pray that your spouse will be obedient to God in the area of giving. After all, we do have a God that answers prayers.

Furthermore, it may take a long, long time before your spouse feels comfortable with any of the family money going to a church. Understandable if the spouse doesn't believe in God. But is there a possibility that she would be willing to support another cause financially, a cause that you both can agree with? For example, is there a Christian homeless ministry that helps people's spiritual and physical needs? Though your spouse may not be willing to give to a church, perhaps they would be willing to give to this?

I believe anytime someone encounters the joy of giving they will be changed. I encourage you to be working towards being able to support the church you go to, but if your spouse is not on board, consider finding an organization that both honors Christ and performs a community service that your spouse can proudly support.

Psalm 34:8 says, *Oh, taste and see that the Lord is good.* Introduce your spouse to the idea that God has a purpose for the way you use your money. Beginning to give *anything, anywhere,* may be just what they need to taste and see a better way to use money. This may be just the stepping-stone they need to fully trust God with their money.

Should I tithe before or after taxes?

In some ways this question doesn't sound like a big deal. However, when you do the math, tithing before or after taxes actually adds up to be a lot of money - especially in the course of a year.

Before going any further on this topic, I want to bring up two things. First, do you want your government to dictate how much money you do, or do not, give to God? If you don't, then please give before taxes are taken out. If you give after taxes are taken out, then you are allowing your government to take the first cut, and then you give what is left afterwards. That might sound a bit abrupt. Don't get me wrong, I happily pay taxes. After all, I like roads, and fire protection, etc. But, when we give based upon how much is left after taxes, we are allowing our government to set how much they get, and then in course, how much we give back to God. When we give first, we are saying, "This is how much I'm giving to God. Then taxes come out; then I live on what's left."

Second, throughout the Scripture we hear about the *firstfuits*. It's the idea that we give to God first, and then live off the rest. Contrast that with, we use our money for taxes, living expenses, needs, wants, etc., *then* we give once all bills are paid. This latter approach doesn't strengthen our faith like it does when we give first. I would encourage you to give before taxes are taken out.

When I first began to wrestle with what I should do, I began to read and pray on the topic. I encourage you to do the same so that this decision can be your own. For me, however, the bottom line came down to one thing. If I have to err on the side of stingy or on the side of generous towards God, I *always* want to err on the side of generous. I don't think I need to give a reason why that is true, but here's the reason. When I was far from God and didn't yet know I needed a Savior, He gave me His most generous present, His Son.

God has always given me the best of Himself. Why would I ever want to do any different? Ephesians 5:1 says, *Be imitators of God as dear children.* Just like children watch and observe their parents, we should do the same by observing our Heavenly Father and doing as He does. God gives me His best, and I want to give Him my best. I tithe on what I make before taxes are taken out because that is the more generous amount.

Once I've decided to give, how, when, and where do I give?

At most churches there are several ways to give. The most common ways are online giving through your church's website, giving on Sunday during the time of offering, or having checks automatically sent to your church from your bank. From the church's perspective, either having checks automatically sent to your church or setting up an ACH recurring payment (usually done through the church's online giving website) is the best way to avoid having your church pay hefty credit card transaction fees. ACH is where you authorize the church to debit your checking/saving account. Setting up automated giving is a great option because if you have to miss going to your church's weekend service, you don't have to worry about how to get your tithe to the church.

Furthermore, if you miss a Sunday service where you normally give your tithe, be sure you don't forget about your gift the next time you are in town. Many times a church's ministry suffers because people simply forget to give their gifts.

They had good intentions, but didn't follow through. It can happen to any of us, but try to stay faithful in your regular giving if you choose to not automate your gift.

The easiest way not to forget is to automate your giving. Most churches provide ways you can give automatic recurring gifts through the methods we just discussed, such as credit/debit cards and ACH. Also, many people can set their banks to automatically send a check to the church at a certain time each month. This service is usually offered for free by your bank. You don't even have to pay for the stamp. If giving is important to you, as it should be, I really want to encourage you to automate it.

Why Ten Percent?

Throughout this book we've talked about the tithe. The tithe means giving ten percent of your income to God. When we read through the many Scriptures that talk about money, we see that God is more concerned about our heart than with what percentage of our income we give away. Still, as we start thinking practically about how we can honor God with our finances, ten percent is a great place to start. This is because the tithe is referenced so many times throughout the Bible. In fact, you won't see any other percentage mentioned. The only percentage we see is the ten percent.

Furthermore, using the tithe gives us a benchmark to make sure we are giving proportionate to what we make. For example, someone who puts ten dollars in the offering plate each week though he is making a six figure salary may think he is generous. However, if you step back, you realize that he is giving very little based upon what he is *capable* of giving. Likewise, a student or someone unemployed giving the same amount may be very generous, and giving sacrificially.

In 1 Corinthians 16:2 Paul says, *On the first day of every week, each of you is to put something aside and store it up, as he may prosper, so that there will be no collecting when I come.* When Paul says, *as he may prosper,* he is saying that our giving should be proportionate to our income. Being generous and giving generously are not a set amount. You could not say that if you give ten thousand dollars a year you are automatically a generous person. Giving that much would be impossible by some and too easy for others. This is why throughout the Bible we see a percentage, not a set amount as how much we should give.

To most people just starting to give to God, ten percent seems like too great a challenge. No matter how tight your budget is, I believe that God's promises could not be more clear that He will provide for your needs. Sure, even giving one dollar is a step of faith for some. But my hope for you is that you put your faith into action by bringing to God the full ten percent. I want you to have the faith that grows your trust in God. Trust God to provide for you and see for yourself what it means when God says to *test Him* to see if He will not be faithful in providing.

If you are serious about giving in a way that honors God, you can probably start with ten percent right away. You may find yourself in a situation where you are living on one hundred percent (or more) of your income. Literally one hundred percent of your income goes to the necessities like rent and groceries. Work out a plan on how you can get to a place where you can live on ninety percent. It might require adjusting your budget, but it will be worth it. Remember the promises of God taking care of you, and move forward with a plan to begin giving ten percent.

When I think about giving, why do I feel scared?

When you begin to think about giving up control of *anything* in your life, you will always have a voice in the back of your mind telling you everything that could possibly go wrong. At different times in my life, I have decided to stop drinking soda. When I'm in the process of stopping, I am instantly hit with all of the reasons I should keep drinking soda. In the back of my mind I keep hearing "I like soda," or "What's so wrong with a soda every now and then." I begin to think about all of those "great" memories enjoying a cold soda. I can kiss that nice part of my life good-bye. It's crazy how I can get anxiety over something as small and obvious as giving up soda.

There are also times of anxiety when I have to delegate things at my job. I will start to think about all the things that could go wrong. I have to remind myself that if all I have are pessimistic thoughts, I will never make improvements in my life. We start to make positive change when we start thinking about the facts of the situation. If I give up soda, I will be healthier, which is good for my family and me. If I *don't* delegate, I will be the bottleneck, and important things will not get done. In the same way, it is only normal to have reservations about giving up control of your money by beginning to trust God with your resources.

No matter how many concerns you have, when contrasted with the benefits of giving, it should be an easy choice, regardless of your fears. The Bible clearly teaches that God will bless you when you trust Him with your finances (Malachi 3). Jesus even taught that when you give up something for Him, He will bless you in this life and the life to come. God challenges us to *try* to outgive Him. Do not let fear hold you back from experiencing God's best for your life.

How are churches funded?

There is a lot of misunderstanding on this issue. The majority of churches are funded by the people who go there. The money that is collected in the Sunday offering, online giving, and the gifts that come in from the week are what allow the church to function. Churches, except maybe a few rare cases, do not receive much, if any, financial support from a denomination or some wealthy benefactor who left money to the church. God uses people just like you and me to support the ministry of churches. Your giving directly impacts the ministry your church can do.

Hopefully, you are part of a church where your pastor is able to talk openly about what Jesus teaches about giving and money. However, that talk can be difficult because people can be sensitive about their money. Will you make it easier for your church to do the ministry God has called it to do by giving generously? Don't wait for the pastor to teach on giving again, or for the next time the pastor encourages people to give. Begin the journey of honoring God with your money today.

How Recap

❖ Start budgeting in such a way that you can give ten percent of your income back to God.

❖ Seriously consider giving first to the local church you are part of. There is no better organization who can holistically reach a community with the Gospel than the local church.

❖ If you have a spouse that does not approve of giving to a church, seek to give to another organization that both honors God and performs a service that your spouse can support.

❖ Tithe based upon your gross income (amount before taxes are taken out). Not only will this help you give more, but it sets a good precedence of giving your best.

❖ If giving is important to you, then automate the gift using either recurring electronic giving or using your bank's Bill Pay feature to automatically send a check each month.

❖ Your giving directly impacts how much ministry your church can do.

How Discussion Questions

❖ In this chapter what was the most helpful for you?

❖ What case can you make to giving ten percent of your income back to God?

❖ Why should you give to your local church?

❖ What role has your local church had in your life? Out of the list of why the local church is important, what reason stuck out to you as most important?

❖ What is your opinion on the topic of giving before or after taxes? Why?

❖ If you wanted to give, but you had a spouse that didn't want to give, how would you handle that?

❖ What are the advantages to automating your giving using something like electronic giving?

❖ Have you ever felt afraid to trust God with something? What lessons can you learn from that as it relates to trusting God with your money?

❖ How does it make you feel that your giving affects the ministry your church is able to do?

15. **Vanity**

Take time to deliberate; but when the time for action arrives, stop thinking and go in.

-Andrew Jackson

Since you've made it this far in the book, you've read what the Bible says about giving. You've also heard my experience on how giving generously is the right thing to do.

So before going any further, I want to ask, will you commit to giving generously?

Why would you trust Jesus with your life and soul, but not your money? It seems ridiculous, yet so many of us live that way. Unlike the story of the rich young ruler, are you willing to put God above your money? Imagine you were the rich young ruler in the Biblical story. Would you have done what Jesus told you to do? If so, begin to honor God with your money. It will take faith, and sacrifice; but it will be worth it!

I've met people who, after hearing what the Bible says about giving, were ready to begin tithing. These people have come to know that the Bible is trustworthy. Throughout their life, they have had faith in other areas that the Bible teaches, such as forgiveness, love, and hope. Once they hear the Bible teaches about giving and being generous, they move forward knowing that giving is God's will for their life. They've experienced God's faithfulness in other areas, and they have no concerns about God's faithfulness in their finances. To these people, once they hear what the Bible teaches on giving, they are on board and ready to give.

A second group of people realizes that giving is an important virtue. They recognize that they've been given much. They want to help out and give back. But, in this group, they fall short by not giving proportionally or consistently. Perhaps when the offering bucket is passed on Sunday mornings, they put the cash from their pocket in the bucket. Putting the cash from your pocket may be proportionate to your income. What I am describing here, however, is someone who has a normal income but gives five, ten, or twenty dollar when they go to a church service. Again, this group recognizes the importance of giving, but does not give anywhere near ten percent of their income.

I also meet people who are skeptical of giving. Beginning to give for the first time may be a big change for them. Making a decision to give God a tithe is a big decision. There is no doubt about that. Many people are afraid to let go of money because it *will* require faith.

The beauty of God's grace is that whichever group you were in yesterday does not have to determine which group you are in today. Today, choose to honor God with your money.

If you have not yet started honoring God with the first ten percent of your income, will you consider tithing for only three months?

I want you to *taste and see* for yourself that God can be trusted with your money. Give ten percent for three months. I know this is a big ask. But, I can promise you it will be worth any sacrifice that you have to make. At the end of the three months, if God did not prove to be faithful, don't continue to give. If at the end of the three months you don't feel satisfied that you've made a great decision, then at the very least you've supported a church that loves Jesus.

There is nothing wrong with being cautious. However, I can tell you that I have seen people who successfully made the leap from being skeptical to giving generously, and then been blown away at God's provision and faithfulness. All you have to do is trust God. After three months of tithing, your life will be changed.

It will be one of the greatest changes you will ever make. Try it. Your faith will be tested, and it will likely be hard. At the same time, you're going to love it, and in doing so, you will be bringing God glory by living a life of generosity, faith and obedience.

I've been giving ten percent for a long time. What is my next step?

For Kristin and I, as we gave ten percent, not only were we able to make ends meet, but we were actually able to live comfortably. We found that we always had at least a little more than we needed. Likewise, some of you have a similar story. You've been giving ten percent for a long time. That is where Kristin and I found ourselves. Tithing in our lives actually became routine. It no longer took faith to believe that God would provide for us as we lived on ninety percent of our income because God continued to allow our income to increase.

We heard an amazing story about Rick Warren and how he and his wife decided they would give an extra one percent of their income each year they were married. Their first year of marriage they gave ten percent. On every wedding anniversary they gave an additional percent back to God. We liked the idea so much we decided to do the same. Each year at our anniversary we increase our giving by one percentage point, which causes us to learn to trust God even more.

Maybe you find yourself in a similar place. Giving and faith are similar to exercising with weights. In order to build muscle you have to increase resistance and add weight. Maybe your faith is getting to the point where you need to add a little extra weight. If once you've been giving for a while and God has blessed you with additional resources to the point that ten percent no longer takes faith, don't stop at ten percent. Keep giving. As Malachi 3 says, *put me to the test, says the Lord of hosts, if I will not open the windows of heaven for you and pour down for you a blessing until there is no more need.*

Kristin and I have put God to the test by trusting Him with our resources and He has been incredibly faithful. I have learned that God *can* be trusted in what He teaches us through the Bible about giving and money. Not only have we seen God prove Himself faithful, but also a lot of good has been done. Lots of people have been pointed to Jesus. And just as I learned first hand about giving from my father and his father, I want our children to grow up experiencing the blessing, joy, and peace that accompanies trusting God with our money.

No matter where you are in the journey of giving, I want to encourage you with a quote from Leonardo da Vinci, *I have been impressed with the urgency of doing. Knowing is not enough; we must apply. Being willing is not enough; we must do.* Don't wait until tomorrow. Now is the time to give generously.

Vanity Recap

❖ As you sacrifice to give generously to God, you will see that your needs are supplied.

❖ If you've never given ten percent of your income, put a date on your calendar where you will give ten percent of your income for three months.

❖ Do not be surprised when what used to take great faith will eventually become easier and easier.

❖ As giving becomes routine, consider increasing your giving so that you can continue to grow in faith while at the same time able to divert more resources to things that truly matter.

❖ Consider setting a date on your calendar, such as an anniversary, where you regularly increase your giving.

Vanity Discussion Questions

❖ In this chapter what was the most helpful for you?

❖ Has there ever been a time in your life when you trusted God with something other than money? What was the result?

❖ Why would giving ten percent for three months be a good way to *taste and see* that God can be trusted?

❖ What is keeping you back from being more generous?

❖ If you currently give ten percent, why would increasing your giving be a good idea?

❖ Is it possible to outgive God? Why, or why not?

❖ What are the most important ways you spend your money?

❖ How can you leverage what is temporary for the sake of what is eternal?

16. **In.**

The kingdom of heaven is like treasure hidden in a field, which a man found and covered up. Then in his joy he goes and sells all that he has and buys that field.

- Jesus, *Matthew* 13:44

I love the above parable. Imagine one day you decided that you would like to buy land. So you begin to search online for nearby land for sell. Occasionally, you find one that seems to be what you are looking for so you drive there and take a closer look at the land. So far you've seen a few things that look good, but you haven't found that perfect spot yet. One day you notice an ad that looks exactly what you're looking for! Exactly! It's too expensive. But you reason to yourself, *I'm just going to go take a look at it. Besides, it is beautiful!* You hop into your car and go see the place. You pull over to the side of the road, and there is no fence, and you don't see anyone around. You convince yourself just to have a look around. You can't afford it, but since you've come this far...

As you're walking around, you see

something twenty yards or so up ahead. A beam of reflected light is coming from the ground. You predict it'll be an old glass bottle someone littered. You walk closer. It's a vein of gold protruding from the ground. You reason that it wouldn't be right to grab as much gold as you can fit into your pockets. After all, this isn't your land. You decide to leave the gold, but you move very quickly to try to buy the land – and thus the gold on the land.

You immediately run back to your car, call your real estate agent, and tell her you'll take the land. You also tell her to sell your current home. The entire car ride back home you think to yourself how are you going to pay for this? You convince yourself that you'll do anything to get that land - because of the gold. You log on to your retirement account, and you cash it all out (yes, even taking the ten percent early withdrawal penalty!), you immediately start putting things up for sale online - your second car, your first car, your furniture. Everything. You begin to pace back and forth in your kitchen. You call your realtor back and tell her, *I've got to get that land.*

And Jesus said, so it is with the Kingdom of Heaven.

Go all in.

If you've decided to follow Jesus, don't honor Him with everything except your money. In the parable, Jesus didn't say he sold some of his stuff and bought the field. He sold everything.

Now it's time to do it. Put this book down. Go to your computer and set up a giving account with your church. Or, go to your drawer and get your checkbook. Go ahead and write out your first check. Don't put it off any longer. You know what God's will is. Don't wait until tomorrow to be obedient. Do it today.

I've explained to you every single reason why I personally give. I hope it made sense. Now, today, it's time for this book not to be why we give, but rather, to be why you give.

Go.
Give Generously.
You know why.

In. Recap

❖ Go all in and follow Jesus. That includes following Jesus with your money.

❖ Begin today to give generously.

❖ Put this book down and take your next step in giving generously.

In. Discussion Questions

❖ What is my next step in giving generously?

❖ Out of all the reasons listed in this book to give, what was the most important reason to you? Why?

❖ How will you begin, or continue, to give generously?

Request for Feedback

If you read this book and were not convinced that giving generously is for you, would you be willing to email me at timothy.milner@gmail.com? I would love to hear from you. Any insights on why you are unconvinced to give would be very valuable to me. Don't worry, I won't try to debate you. I simply want to understand how you think about giving. It might seem inconsequential to you, but I would receive your comments and concerns as a great gift.

Appx: **Biblical**

Biblical Passages with Commentary
58 Relevant Passages on Giving

Genesis 14:20

...and blessed be God Most High, who has delivered your enemies into your hand! And Abram gave him a tenth of everything.

Abraham knew that God had given him victory, and because God gave him victory, Abraham recognized that the riches and wealth he gained from over taking the army were a direct result of God's blessing. So, what did Abraham do? He gave ten percent of it to the high priest of the time, Melchizedek, and by doing so he gave to God.

Leviticus 25:23

The land shall not be sold in perpetuity, for the land is mine. For you are strangers and sojourners with me.

When someone "bought" land, they were simply buying the right to use the land. This is a great verse to think through the concept that we are stewards – not owners – of all that we possess.

Leviticus 27:3

Every tithe of the land, whether of the seed of the land or of the fruit of the trees, is the Lord's; it is holy to the Lord

In order for the Israelites to remember that *everything* they had came from God, God told them that one tenth of all things shall be dedicated to God, and declared holy. Essentially, God tells us that He has given us everything that we have. In order to acknowledge that God has given us all that we have, we are told to dedicate ten percent of it to God and to give it back to Him.

Deuteronomy 8:18

You shall remember the Lord your God, for it is he who gives you power to get wealth, that he may confirm his covenant that he swore to your fathers, as it is this day.

Have you considered where your ideas, ambitions, opportunities, and even the thoughts that lead to your success come from? God gives us these things! So do not take the stance that everything you have, you've earned. It's simply not the full story. You've been given much.

Deuteronomy 14:27-29

And you shall not neglect the Levite who is within your towns, for he has no portion or inheritance with you. At the end of every three years you shall bring out all the tithe of your produce in the same year and lay it up within your towns. And the Levite, because he has no portion or inheritance with you, and the sojourner, the fatherless, and the widow, who are within your towns, shall come and eat and be filled, that the Lord your God may bless you in all the work of your hands that you do.

The Israelites were required to bring a tithe every third year to assist with the Levities (similar to the clergy today) and the poor. The point is that the Israelites were told that everything they had was from God and that a portion of it was to be made holy and given back to God. Furthermore, one application for us today is that God loves to use the Church to serve the Church. Be generous towards the church you attend and look for ways to help those in need and those who rely on donations to continue their ministry work.

Deuteronomy 15: 7-11

If among you, one of your brothers should become poor, in any of your towns within your land that the Lord your God is giving you, you shall not harden your heart or shut your hand against your poor brother, but you shall open your hand to him and lend him sufficient for his need, whatever it may be. Take care lest there be an unworthy thought in your heart... and your eye look grudgingly on your poor brother, and you give him nothing, and he cry to the Lord against you, and you be guilty of sin. You shall give to him freely, and your heart shall not be grudging when you give to him, because for this the Lord your God will bless you in all your work and in all that you undertake. For there will never cease to be poor in the land. Therefore I command you, "You shall open wide your hand to your brother, to the needy and to the poor, in your land."

This is a great Old Testament passage about how the Israelites were to help their fellow Israelites in times of need. The principle for the Church today still stands. Be on the lookout for ways to help.

2 Kings 4:8-17

One day Elisha went on to Shunem, where a wealthy woman lived, who urged him to eat some food. So whenever he passed that way, he would turn in there to eat food. And she said to her husband, "Behold now, I know that this is a holy man of God who is continually passing our way. Let us make a small room on the roof with walls and put there for him a bed, a table, a chair, and a lamp, so that whenever he comes to us, he can go in there."

One day he came there, and he turned into the chamber and rested there. And he said to Gehazi his servant, "Call this Shunammite." When he had called her, she stood before him. And he said to him, "Say now to her, 'See, you have taken all this trouble for us; what is to be done for you? Would you have a word spoken on your behalf to the king or to the commander of the army?'" She answered, "I dwell among my own people." And he said, "What then is to be done for her?" Gehazi answered, "Well, she has no son, and her husband is old." He said, "Call her." And when he had called her, she stood in the doorway. And he said, "At this season, about this time next year, you shall embrace a son." And she said, "No, my lord, O man of God; do not lie to your servant." But the woman conceived, and she bore a son about that time the following spring, as Elisha had said to her.

In this account, we see that God did not bless this wealthy woman with more money; at least not initially. Rather God blessed this woman and her husband with a child. They had wanted a child but the woman was barren.

I believe this would be a good time to add that the woman had God's favor, but not because she gave. The woman had God's favor, because she loved and sought after God. Because the woman loved God, of course she gave generously.

She understood that out of all the things she could give her money to, she wanted to first give back to God. Jesus said where our treasure is, there our heart will be also (Matthew 6:21).

She gave because she loved God. From what we see in the passage, I'm willing to bet that even if she was not given a child, saved from the famine, or found favor with the king, she would still love God, and she would still continue to give generously towards the God she loved so much.

Nonetheless, this is a thought provoking Biblical account of someone being blessed because they were faithful in providing for those who serve God.

Psalms 40:8

I delight to do Your will, O my God; Your Law is within my heart.

If it is true that you delight to do the will of God, are you delighted to live a life of generosity knowing that it will require sacrifice? Perhaps the first question should be to ask why we delight to do God's will. One of the reasons is that when we've done God's will in the past, we've experienced the joy of doing what God asks us to do. In the same way, we know that the next time we do it God's way, we will experience the same joy. If you've delighted to follow God's way in the area of, for example, forgiving someone, trust me when I say you will also be delighted to follow God's way in the area of giving.

Psalms 81:11-13

But my people did not listen to my voice; Israel would not submit to me. So I gave them over to their stubborn hearts, to follow their own counsels. Oh, that my people would listen to me, that Israel would walk in my ways!

A warning to those who do not submit to God's will. While there are many Scriptures that talk about God being slow to anger, His steadfast love, mercies and grace, we should not deceive ourselves that whatever we decide to do is fine and there will be no consequence even if we decide to disobey God.

Psalm 143:10

Teach me to do Your will, For You are my God; Let Your good Spirit lead me on level ground.

One component of learning to do God's will is to study the Bible. One component of studying the Bible is to be honest when we come across passages that contradict our actions. When you see a passage that seems to be suggesting that God's way is different than your way, take the time to carefully study the passage's meaning and how it should be applied today.

Proverbs 3:9-10

Honor the Lord with your wealth and with the firstfruits of all your produce; then your barns will be filled with plenty, and your vats will be bursting with wine.

The firstfruits were exactly what they sound like – the first fruits of the season. Applying this today, don't wait until the end of the month or year to give God out of what's left of your extra resources. Make it a routine to give to God first; not after all other needs and desires have been satisfied.

Kristin and I make it a point to tithe on our income the moment it comes in. We used to wait until the end of the month, but after studying the passages in the Bible where it talks about first fruits, I wanted to go ahead and give immediately after receiving income.

Proverbs 19:17

Whoever is generous to the poor lends to the Lord, and he will repay him for his deed.

We see a theme throughout the Bible that we should give to those who are unable to pay us back. Christ gave us a gift that we will never be able to repay – His life for ours ultimately portrays this. This verse tells us that when we do give to one who cannot pay us back, it is the Lord who will pay us back.

Malachi 3:8-12

Can a person rob God? You indeed are robbing me, but you say, "How are we robbing you?" In tithes and contributions! You are bound for judgment because you are robbing me – this whole nation is guilty. "Bring the entire tithe into the storehouse so that there may be food in my temple. Test me in this matter," says the Lord who rules over all, "to see if I will not open for you the windows of heaven and pour out for you a blessing until there is no room for it all. Then I will stop the plague from ruining your crops, and the vine will not lose its fruit before harvest," says the Lord who rules over all. "All nations will call you happy, for you indeed will live in a delightful land," says the Lord who rules over all.

This is the only time throughout the Bible that God says in a *positive* way, *test me.* He is saying bring your full tithe and *test me, To see if I will not open for you the windows of heaven and pour out for you a blessing until there is no room for it all.* If I had a friend who gave me the same challenge, you better believe that I would take him up on this offer. I'm sure you'd probably do the same. So, of course, let's take our Heavenly Father up on this offer as well! Remember also, that it's not that God needs our gifts. God designed us. He knows us, and He knows that when we give it is healthy for us. It helps us to take on more of the character of Jesus.

Matthew 2:11

And going into the house they saw the child with Mary his mother, and they fell down and worshiped him. Then, opening their treasures, they offered him gifts, gold and frankincense and myrrh.

Giving is a form of worship as well. When we give a gift that requires great sacrifice, it communicates that the recipient is worth it. What should it tell us when we think about Jesus giving His life for us? What should we think about the gifts we give to God?

Matthew 5:16

...let your light shine before others, so that they may see your good works and give glory to your Father who is in heaven.

God uses giving to draw glory to Himself. A watching world often has no idea what compels Christians to give. And when people who do not know God see Christians sacrificially giving, it can often times spark questions of curiosity.

Matthew 5:21-22

You have heard that it was said to those of old, "You shall not murder; and whoever murders will be liable to judgment." But I say to you that everyone who is angry with his brother will be liable to judgment.

Here, Jesus is saying that now that we are under the law of grace, the standard is actually higher.

Jesus says the requirement used to be that you don't murder, but now I don't want you to even stay angry with each other. Jesus goes on to other subjects such as adultery and says that the standard used to be don't commit adultery, now the standard is don't even have an adulterous thought. With the freedom that Jesus has given us also comes greater responsibility.

Unfortunately, there are some who suggest now that Jesus has come we no longer have to give back to God and that we can keep all of our money for ourselves. But using this passage as an example, I would say the opposite is true. Now that Christ has come and set us free, less is not required, but rather more.

Matthew 5:42

Give to the one who begs from you, and do not refuse the one who would borrow from you.

Always be prepared to help. As stated earlier in this book, giving cash to someone who begs is not always the best way to give. In your context determine what the best way is to help someone who begs from you. From this passage it seems pretty clear that Jesus intends us to help those who beg, and we should not dismiss it. There are ways to give to them without handing them cash.

Matthew 6:1-4

Beware of practicing your righteousness before

other people in order to be seen by them, for then you will have no reward from your Father who is in heaven. Thus, when you give to the needy, sound no trumpet before you, as the hypocrites do in the synagogues and in the streets, that they may be praised by others. Truly, I say to you, they have received their reward. But when you give to the needy, do not let your left hand know what your right hand is doing, so that your giving may be in secret. And your Father who sees in secret will reward you.

Here's one note on how *not* to give to the poor! People like to be seen as generous. It is an attractive quality. Think about the people you see as generous. Do you wish others saw you in the same light? Naturally, most of us would have to be honest and answer that question with a yes. However, we can short circuit the way God designed us when we advertise ourselves as being generous. If at some point you are giving so people see you as generous, stop what you are doing. Something has gone awry.

Let's talk quickly about motives. Don't let your fear of having the wrong motive keep you from doing the right thing. I've heard people say they don't want to do something that is indeed a good thing, because they weren't sure if they had the right motive. Move forward with doing the right thing. But, be sure focus on having pure motives. For example, don't *avoid* giving because you are afraid it will go to your head. Instead, give, but take effort to be sure you give with pure motives.

Matthew 6:10

Your kingdom come. Your will be done, On earth as it is in heaven.

Christ is teaching us to seek God's will for all areas of our life - including His will for how we are to give generously. Just like the story of the rich young ruler, don't seek to honor God in all areas of your life *except* with your money. Let us use the resources that God has blessed us with to usher in God's Kingdom on earth as it is heaven. How do we do this? We give towards things that teach Christ. We help the poor. We live life open handed.

Matthew 6:19-21

Do not lay up for yourselves treasures on earth, where moth and rust destroy and where thieves break in and steal, but lay up for yourselves treasures in heaven, where neither moth nor rust destroys and where thieves do not break in and steal. For where your treasure is, there your heart will be also.

If you want to know what your heart is connected to, take a look at your last bank statement. You spend your money on the things you value the most. If you love to look good, you're going to see you bought a lot of clothes. If you love to be entertained, you're going to see you spent a lot on entertainment. If you love knowledge and learning, you'll probably see you bought a lot of books. But what does it mean when you look at your bank statement and you gave nothing or very little of what you made to God? Seriously, what does that mean? Does it even matter?

Riches of this world are terribly short lived. This is especially true in light of eternity. Jesus is begging the question, why build up wealth here on earth when you can use that same money to build up wealth in heaven.

Matthew 10:39

Whoever finds his life will lose it, and whoever loses his life for my sake will find it

The same is true with being generous. Just like Jesus said you can't know *true* life until you lose your old life, the same is true today with being generous. You can't know what it's like to be right with God with your finances without first giving generously.

Matthew 13:44

The kingdom of heaven is like treasure hidden in a field, which a man found and covered up. Then in his joy he goes and sells all that he has and buys that field.

Following God in all areas of our life is worth it.

There is no expense too great; fear too strong; challenge too complex, when it comes to honoring God in all areas of our life.

Matthew 25:14-30

For it will be like a man going on a journey, who called his servants and entrusted to them his property. To one he gave five talents, to another two, to another one, to each according to his ability. Then he went away. He who had received the five talents went at once and traded with them, and he made five talents more. So also he who had the two talents made two talents more. But he who had received the one talent went and dug in the ground and hid his master's money. Now after a long time the master of those servants came and settled accounts with them. And he who had received the five talents came forward, bringing five talents more, saying, "Master, you delivered to me five talents; here I have made five talents more." His master said to him, "Well done, good and faithful servant. You have been faithful over a little; I will set you over much. Enter into the joy of your master." And he also who had the two talents came forward, saying, "Master, you delivered to me two talents; here I have made two talents more." His master said to him, "Well done, good and faithful servant. You have been faithful over a little; I will set you over much. Enter into the joy of your master." He also who had received the one talent came forward, saying, "Master, I knew you to be a hard man, reaping where you did not sow, and gathering where you scattered no seed, so I was afraid, and I went and hid your talent in the ground. Here you have what is yours." But his master answered him, "You wicked and slothful servant! You knew that I reap where I have not sown and gather where I scattered no seed? Then you ought to have invested my money with the bankers, and at my coming I should have received what was my own with interest. So take the talent from him and give it to him who has the ten talents. For to everyone who has will more be given, and he will have an abundance. But from the one who has not, even what he has will be taken away. And cast the worthless servant into the outer darkness. In that place there will be weeping and gnashing of teeth."

This passage teaches us some very important lessons about stewarding (whatever it is that we steward): a) God has given us so much! Keep in mind here that a talent is about 50 years wages. b) God has given us different amounts to steward c) Everything we steward comes from the Master. d) We are given a great deal of freedom to steward how we see fit. e) God will one day have us give an account of how we steward what He gave us. f) There will be blessings for those who steward well. g) There will be punishment for those who do not steward well.

    We are told that those who did a good job were faithful with what they were given. We are told that they multiplied what they were given. Finally, they gave their master a good return on his investment. We are faithful, we multiply and provide a good return on investment when we invest what God has given us into things that build God's Kingdom.

Matthew 25:35-40

For I was hungry and you gave me food, I was thirsty and you gave me drink, I was a stranger and you welcomed me, I was naked and you clothed me, I was sick and you visited me, I was in prison and you came to me. Then the righteous will answer him, saying, "Lord, when did we see you hungry and feed you, or thirsty and give you drink? And when did we see you a stranger and welcome you, or naked and clothe you? And when did we see you sick or in prison and visit you?" And the King will answer them, "Truly, I say to you, as you did it to one of the least of these my brothers, you did it to me."

If we look for opportunities to give, we will see that opportunities are all around us.

Mark 10:17-27

And as he was setting out on his journey, a man ran up and knelt before him and asked him, "Good Teacher, what must I do to inherit eternal life?" And Jesus said to him, "Why do you call me good? No one is good except God alone. You know the commandments: 'Do not murder, Do not commit adultery, Do not steal, Do not bear false witness, Do not defraud, Honor your father and mother.'" And he said to him, "Teacher, all these I have kept from my youth." And Jesus, looking at him, loved him, and said to him, "You lack one thing: go, sell all that you have and give to the poor, and you will have treasure in heaven; and come, follow me." Disheartened by the saying, he went away sorrowful, for he had great possessions.

And Jesus looked around and said to his disciples, "How difficult it will be for those who have wealth to enter the kingdom of God!" And the disciples were amazed at his words. But Jesus said to them again, "Children, how difficult it is to enter the kingdom of God! It is easier for a camel to go through the eye of a needle than for a rich person to enter the kingdom of God." And they were exceedingly astonished, and said to him, "Then who can be saved?" Jesus looked at them and said, "With man it is impossible, but not with God. For all things are possible with God."

Jesus tells him to sell all that he has and give it to the poor. Some things in the Bible are descriptive and some are prescriptive. In other words, there are parts of the Bible that teach us what we need to do. This would be prescriptive. There are other parts of the Bible where we are simply told what happened. These things are descriptive and we do not necessarily need to do them today.

However, we should take note, because they are filled with lessons that are applicable for us today. Most people today would agree that the story of Jesus and the rich young ruler is descriptive. It's not necessarily saying everyone must take a vow of poverty. However, if money is your god, the only way to make God your only true God may be a dramatic action like selling all you have and giving it away. Maybe the question for you is not, are you willing to give away everything, but rather, are you willing to give away *anything*?

Mark 10:28-30

Peter began to say to him, "See, we have left everything and followed you." Jesus said, "Truly, I say to you, there is no one who has left house or brothers or sisters or mother or father or children or lands, for my sake and for the gospel, who will not receive a hundredfold now in this time, houses and brothers and sisters and mothers and children and lands, with persecutions, and in the age to come eternal life."

In this passage Peter is telling Jesus that he has given up everything to follow Jesus. Peter had left the family business, and his home. What does Jesus say when he hears Peter say this? He says you are going to be blessed in a big way in this life and in the life to come.

Luke 11:42

But woe to you Pharisees! For you tithe mint and rue and every herb, and neglect justice and the love of God. These you ought to have done, without neglecting the others.

When talking to the Pharisees, Jesus calls the Pharisees out as hypocrites. The Pharisees were great at tithing and following rules, but they were terrible at the more important things such as justice and loving God. Jesus tells them that they did right to tithe, but they should have tithed while also doing the more important things.

Luke 12:13-21

Someone in the crowd said to him, "Teacher, tell my brother to divide the inheritance with me." But he said to him, "Man, who made me a judge or arbitrator over you?" And he said to them, "Take care, and be on your guard against all covetousness, for one's life does not consist in the abundance of his possessions." And he told them a parable, saying, "The land of a rich man produced plentifully, and he thought to himself, 'What shall I do, for I have nowhere to store my crops?' And he said, 'I will do this: I will tear down my barns and build larger ones, and there I will store all my grain and my goods. And I will say to my soul, 'Soul, you have ample goods laid up for many years; relax, eat, drink, be merry.'" But God said to him, "Fool! This night your soul is required of you, and the things you have prepared, whose will they be?" So is the one who lays up treasure for himself and is not rich toward God.

The rich man in this parable was wealthy. Very wealthy. He had everything he needed. So much so that he had to keep building bigger barns just to store it all. But, and this is a big but, he was not rich towards God. Presumably, because he hoarded all of his money for himself. And when his time had come and he died here on earth, all his wealth - everything he had lived for - was left behind. Perhaps this is where the phrase, "You can't take it with you when you die" originated.

Luke 16:1-13

He also said to the disciples, "There was a rich man who had a manager, and charges were brought to him that this man was wasting his possessions. And he called him and said to him, 'What is this that I hear about you? Turn in the account of your management, for you can no longer be manager.' And the manager said to himself, 'What shall I do, since my master is taking the management away from me? I am not strong enough to dig, and I am ashamed to beg. I have decided what to do, so that when I am removed from management, people may receive me into their houses.' So, summoning his master's debtors one by one, he said to the first, 'How much do you owe my master?' He said, 'A hundred measures of oil.' He said to him, 'Take your bill, and sit down quickly and write fifty.' Then he said to another, 'And how much do you owe?' He said, 'A hundred measures of wheat.' He said to him, 'Take your bill, and write eighty.' The master commended the dishonest manager for his shrewdness. For the sons of this world are more shrewd in dealing with their own generation than the sons of light. And I tell you, make friends for yourselves by means of unrighteous wealth, so that when it fails they may receive you into the eternal dwellings."

One who is faithful in a very little is also faithful in much, and one who is dishonest in a very little is also dishonest in much. If then you have not been faithful in the unrighteous wealth, who will entrust to you the true riches? And if you have not been faithful in that which is another's, who will give you that which is your own? No servant can serve two masters, for either he will hate the one and love the other, or he will be devoted to the one and despise the other. You cannot serve God and money.

This is perhaps my favorite passage on giving in the Bible. The first part of the passage is this amazing story where the point is that we should be strategic in how we spend our money. Essentially, we see people being creative in solving all types of problems that ultimately don't even matter. Yet, for the things that truly matter, like telling people about Jesus, we use almost no creativity at all. Why is that? Jesus says that is not good. We should give the best of ourselves to solving the most important problems.

The second part of this passage is telling us that we cannot seek to honor God and money. We have to pick one. For example, if you love money, you will see that when a choice is made, you will choose your money over God. If you choose God, then you will see that your money is used to serve God. Which path are you choosing?

Luke 21:1-4

Jesus looked up and saw the rich putting their gifts into the offering box, and he saw a poor widow put in two small copper coins. And he said, "Truly, I tell you, this poor widow has put in more than all of them. For they all contributed out of their abundance, but she out of her poverty put in all she had to live on."

Let your giving, no matter the size, serve as a sign of your faith. Are you a stay-at-home-mom and you want to give, but you have no income, and your husband is not on board with giving? Give on what you do make or are given such as a clothing allowance. It truly may only be a few dollars here and there, but the size of the gift does not matter. The lady in this passage gave less than a modern day penny, yet Jesus praised her generosity.

John 6:27

Do not work for the food that perishes, but for the food that endures to eternal life...

Yes, we can spend everything we earn on "food," (anything that is temporary). Or, we can leverage as much as we can on the *food that endures to eternal life.* Which one do you think is the better investment?

Romans 11:16

If the dough offered as firstfruits is holy, so is the whole lump, and if the root is holy, so are the branches.

Do we have to give away everything we own to be right with God in our finances? For most of us, the answer would be no. Of course we see things like the story of the rich young ruler and we all get nervous thinking God may be telling us to do the same. If you are supposed to give everything away, God will make that clear, if you are listening. However, most of the time, we are allowed to steward what we've been given. And we've been given a great deal of freedom in how we are to steward.

As long as you are giving proportionally of your income (tithing), then yes, you are honoring God with your finances. Unless of course, God has made it clear to you that you should give over and beyond your tithe. If someone decided to give away everything for God's glory, I believe that could be a wonderful act of worship and faith. However, I don't see that as a requirement throughout the Scriptures. What I do see is a requirement to give back the first ten percent. When we do that, we honor God with our finances, or as this passage says, when we give back the first part to God, then the whole is made holy (or set apart for God).

Romans 11:36

For from him and through him and to him are all things. To him be glory forever. Amen.

All things are Christ's. He made them, He sustains them, and all things belong to Him. We simply steward the things He has given us.

Romans 12:2

And do not be conformed to this world, but be transformed by the renewing of your mind, so that you may prove what the will of God is, that which is good and acceptable and perfect.

As we submit to Christ and His will, over time we will become more like Him. As we become more like Him we will increasingly learn that His ways are good, acceptable and perfect. This is equally true for learning that God's design for how we will steward our financial resources is *good*.

Romans 15:26

For Macedonia and Achaia have been pleased to make some contribution for the poor among the saints at Jerusalem.

Keep your ears and eyes open to how God wants to use you. Perhaps there are needs in your own house that you can help with. Maybe there are needs in your neighborhood, or perhaps there are needs on the other side of the world. Pray that God would use you in whatever way – small or big.

1 Corinthians 6:19-20

Or do you not know that your body is a temple of the Holy Spirit within you, whom you have from God? You are not your own, for you were bought with a price. So glorify God in your body.

Well at least I own *me*? Not so fast. Your body is a temple for the Holy Spirit. Christ has bought you with a great price. Even your life is Christ's. We are simply stewards of what God has loaned us.

1 Corinthians 7:29

For the present form of this world is passing away.

Life on earth is very short. It would be unwise to only think about the here and now. We should think from time to time about the end. If I continue to do what I'm doing today, for the rest of my life, will it get me where I want to be ultimately? What decisions have you made based upon the fact that life is short? Where are you storing your treasure (earth or heaven)?

1 Corinthians 13:3

If I give away all I have, and if I deliver up my body to be burned, but have not love, I gain nothing.

It's not *just* about giving. It's just as much about *why* we give. Our giving needs to be motivated by love. God loves us and He gave his only Son to save us from our sins. It's that love that should motivate us to give.

1 Corinthians 16:2

On the first day of every week, each of you is to put something aside and store it up, as he may prosper, so that there will be no collecting when I come.

When Paul says, *as he may prosper,* he is saying that our giving should be proportionate to our income. Being generous and giving generously are not a set amount. You could not say that if you give ten thousand dollars a year you are automatically a generous person. Giving that much would be impossible by some and too easy for others. This is why throughout the Bible we see a tithe, or ten percent, not a set amount as how much we should give.

2 Corinthians 9:6

The point is this: whoever sows sparingly will also

reap sparingly, and whoever sows bountifully will also reap bountifully.

If you only invest a little, your reward will be little. Don't let this surprise you. It's a universal law. Let's say you know of a new company that is about to do great things. So, you decide to buy their stock. If you invest $100, your reward is going to be relatively small compared to if you invested $10,000. The same is true to how much we invest into God's Kingdom. Again, it's not about the size of the gift, but rather by the size of the sacrifice.

2 Corinthians 9:7

Each one must give as he has decided in his heart, not reluctantly or under compulsion, for God loves a cheerful giver...

Give some time thinking about your giving strategy. Don't decide last minute to give more or less than you were planning. For example, while at church if you weren't planning on giving anything that particular Sunday, don't start to panic as the offering bucket is coming your way. Let the bucket pass you by! But, take an opportunity after you get home to seriously think about what God would have you to give next Sunday or whatever your case may be.

When you give, give cheerfully! Giving is an incredible opportunity for us. Giving should not be compared to getting a traffic ticket, or getting a root canal, or fixing a flat tire on the side of the highway. If the same emotions from those three things pop up when you think about giving, then you are probably not a cheerful giver.

2 Corinthians 9:10

He who supplies seed to the sower and bread for food will supply and multiply your seed for sowing and increase the harvest of your righteousness.

When you give, God will be pleased. He will likely give you more seed to also sow. In other words, God will bless you in ways so you can increase your giving.

2 Corinthians 9:11a

You will be enriched in every way to be generous in every way,

If you want to be generous, God will help you be generous in every way. When we want to be like God by being generous, God is going to bless that desire. Once you decide to give generously, expect to find many opportunities to do so!

2 Corinthians 9:11b-13

...which through us will produce thanksgiving to God. For the ministry of this service is not only supplying the needs of the saints but is also overflowing in many thanksgivings to God. By

their approval of this service, they will glorify God... and the generosity of your contribution for them and for all others...

Not only is your giving providing for actual needs, but your giving will cause people to be thankful to God. How great is that? You can use your money to help people praise God.

Ephesians 4:18

I have received full payment, and more. I am well supplied, having received from Epaphroditus the gifts you sent, a fragrant offering, a sacrifice acceptable and pleasing to God.

Just like the verse before this one, when we give, not only does it supply strategic needs such as fueling the vision of your church to reach your community for Jesus, but God sees your gift as a *fragrant* offering. Paul tells us in this passage, that your gift is pleasing to God. If you only do one thing today, but that one thing is *pleasing God*, this is going to be a great day!

Ephesians 5:1

Be imitators of God as dear children.

Let's remember that we have a very generous God. He has given us so much, and it's really our privilege to be able to give. As a Christian do we not desire to take on more of the character of God?

Hebrews 13:5

Keep your life free from love of money, and be content with what you have, for he has said, "I will never leave you nor forsake you."

Remember the Parable of the Sower? One of the sown seeds was not fruitful because of the worries of the world and the deceitfulness of riches. If you love money, it will keep you from being fruitful in following Jesus. Perhaps the best anti-venom to becoming a money lover is generosity.

Hebrews 13:6

Do not neglect to do good and to share what you have, for such sacrifices are pleasing to God.

Have you thought about the fact that when you share what you have, it *actually* pleases God? Think about that for a moment – what does it mean to please God? Does God literally smile down on us when we share what we have?

James 2:14-17

What good is it, my brothers, if someone says he has faith but does not have works? Can that faith save him? If a brother or sister is poorly clothed and lacking in daily food, and one of you says to them, "Go in peace, be warmed and filled," without giving them the things needed for the body, what good is that? So also faith by itself, if it does not have works, is dead.

It's an important reminder that we receive salvation (accepted by God) simply by believing Him. We do not have to work to be accepted by God. We simply have to believe He is who He says He is. When we see Him for who He really is, we won't be able to help ourselves but do things that please him - things such as helping people in need. These verses serve as a great reminder that if we say that we love God, yet do nothing for others, then something is wrong in our faith with God. James blatantly says that if that is the case, then your faith is actually dead.

James 4:7

Submit yourselves therefore to God.

Early in the process of deciding to be generous we must ask if we are willing to wholeheartedly submit to God's will for our lives. If you are willing to submit every area of your life to God, then giving will be a natural by-product of your faith. But if you are only willing to submit everything to God *except* your money, you will see that your love of money is keeping you from being fruitful in your faith. See the Parable of the

Sower (Matthew 13:22), and The Rich Young Ruler (Mark 10:17-22).

1 Timothy 5:8

But if anyone does not provide for his relatives, and especially for members of his household, he has denied the faith and is worse than an unbeliever.

If there is a need among our own family, it's our responsibility to help. Could you imagine someone who gives away all they have to a great cause, yet neglects his own family? What would that say about his priorities? What would his or her children grow up thinking about their parents "generosity?"

1 Timothy 5:17-18

You shall not muzzle an ox when it treads out the grain, and, "The laborer deserves his wages."

Christians are to support those whose full time vocation is to advance the Gospel. In most cases, the best way is to support the local church you attend.

1 Timothy 6:10

For the love of money is a root of all kinds of evils. It is through this craving that some have wandered away from the faith and pierced themselves with many pangs.

There are a couple of interesting observations from this passage. First of all, note that it says the *love* of money is the root of all kinds of evil. It does not say that money is the root, but rather the love of it. If you have lots of money, that is not an evil thing. Loving money will lead to trouble – for the wealthy and the poor alike.

Second, there will be many times in life where we face decisions on what is most important to us. There will be times when we have to choose between something that will help our faith but lower our bank account. Likewise, there will be times when we can choose to boost our income, but it will come at a great cost to our faith. It is far better to choose ahead of time what is the most important to you: God or money. Remember that loving God leads to life. Loving money leads to spiritual death.

1 Timothy 6:17-19

As for the rich in this present age, They are to do good, to be rich in good works, to be generous and ready to share, thus storing up treasure for themselves as a good foundation for the future, so that they may take hold of that which is truly life.

By being generous and ready to share you can do just as Jesus taught us by storing for yourselves treasure in heaven. One other note on this passage from 1 Timothy. Paul the author of this passage ends the verse with, *that they may take hold of that which is truly life.* Sound familiar? Paul is echoing Jesus' words in Luke 16 of the true riches.

1 John 2:15-17

Do not love the world or the things in the world. If anyone loves the world, the love of the Father is not in him. For all that is in the world—the desires of the flesh and the desires of the eyes and pride of life—is not from the Father but is from the world. And the world is passing away along with its desires, but whoever does the will of God abides forever.

Don't miss understand this passage. We are supposed to love the world in the sense of loving people and even enjoying creation. The John who wrote this passage is the same John who wrote John 3:16 - *For God so loved the world...* So what does this passage mean for us today? Don't fall in love with the things of this world because it's so temporary. Here John is helping us to have the perspective that this world is temporary - it's just a speck on the continuum of eternity. So, let's do things in this short life that will have a positive impact on eternity.

1 John 3:17

But if anyone has the world's goods and sees his

brother in need, yet closes his heart against him, how does God's love abide in him?

One need that God uses the Church to fulfill is helping other Christians in need.

1 Peter 2:12

...when they speak against you as evildoers, they may see your good deeds and glorify God...
When people find out that you follow Jesus, they may begin to think any number of things about you. Depending on their past experiences with Christians – even if that past experience is only something they've seen on TV or the internet – the way they feel about you may be either negative or positive. However, when someone has a negative view of those who follow Christ, yet know that you care about helping the poor, the needy, and the community in general, that will give you a tremendous amount of good will. I've personally had conversations where I was speaking to someone who did not approve of Christianity, but once he heard that I too have taken action to help others, I could immediately see the walls separating him from the Gospel come crashing down. Let those who disagree with Jesus, be tempted to rethink their stance when they say see our good deeds and let's pray they too glorify God.

1 Peter 5:6

Humble yourselves, therefore, under the mighty hand of God so that at the proper time he may exalt you...

At the end of the day, are you willing to put your financial dreams on hold if that is what necessary for you to honor God with the money that He has entrusted to you? Seriously, think about this. If it means having to put your dream of buying a house (or a bigger house) on hold so that you can at a minimum tithe (give ten percent of your income), are you willing to do that? We must humble ourselves and follow God's design. God intentionally created the entire concept of tithing and being generous. There is a reason He has done so. Are you willing to trust Him that it is for our best?

Tim Milner is the lead pastor at Essential Church (essentialhsv.com) in the downtown area of Huntsville, AL. Previous, Tim was the executive pastor at Epic Church in San Francisco, CA. He and his wonderful wife, Kristin, have two daughters, Sophia and Selah.

If you would like to contact TimMilner, you can email him at timothy.milner@gmail.com.

Tim is committed to helping people understand what the Bible teaches on giving. Generosity has so marked Tim's life that he wants nothing more than to teach people the joy that they can have if they decide to honor God with their money.

If you would like to order additional copies of *Why We Give* for your church, family, or friends, please email timothy.milner@gmail.com for the lowest prices.